STAFFING YOUR
FOODSERVICE OPERATION

FOODSERVICE EMPLOYEE MANAGEMENT SERIES

Retaining Foodservice Employees
Disciplining Foodservice Employees

Staffing Your Foodservice Operation

KAREN EICH DRUMMOND

VNR VAN NOSTRAND REINHOLD
New York

To my little mischief, CAITLIN

Copyright © 1991 by Van Nostrand Reinhold

Library of Congress Catalog Card Number 90-48599
ISBN 0-442-00572-5

Printed in the United States of America.

Van Nostrand Reinhold
115 Fifth Avenue
New York, New York 10003

Chapman and Hall
2-6 Boundary Row
London, SE1 8HN, England

Thomas Nelson Australia
102 Dodds Street
South Melbourne 3205
Victoria, Australia

Nelson Canada
1120 Birchmount Road
Scarborough, Ontario MIK 5G4, Canada

16 15 14 13 12 11 10 9 8 7 6 5 4 3 2 1

Library of Congress Cataloging-in-Publication Data

Drummond, Karen Eich.
    Staffing your foodservice operation / Karen Eich Drummond.
        p. cm.—(Foodservice employee management series)
    Includes bibliographical references and index.
    ISBN 0-442-00572-5
    1. Food service—Personnel management. I. Title. II. Series.
TX911.3.P4D79 1991
674.95´068´3—dc20
                                                    90-48599
                                                    CIP

CONTENTS

PREFACE

The topic of staffing your foodservice operation has become, and will continue to be, a hot topic, in view of the labor shortage, which is not going to improve for some time yet. At the same time that you are having difficulties finding an adequate number of qualified personnel, your operation may also be growing and your guests may be more demanding. So, you may hire more personnel, only to find that some cannot prove eligibility to work in the United States and others do not even stay through the first month. These occurrences are not unusual; they have become part of doing business.

The purpose of this book is to help you step by step through the staffing process of recruiting, evaluating, selecting, and hiring employees. It is written from a practical and concise perspective, and it contains many lists, charts, sample forms, and resources that you can tap for further information. It is written primarily about staffing your operation with hourly or nonexempt employees; however, there are many notes pertaining to salaried or management personnel.

This book is divided into three parts: background information; recruiting; and evaluating, selecting, and hiring. Before delving into staffing, the dynamics of the labor market, job descriptions, and the legal aspects of staffing are discussed in Part One.

Part Two, "Recruiting," goes into detail concerning both traditional and newer sources of applicants, such as the handicapped, and how to reach them. This part also describes prerequisites to recruiting, including incentives foodservice employers are offering, such as training opportunities. There is information on how to develop your own incentive program.

Part Three discusses the how-tos of evaluating applicants through the use of applications, interviews, tests, and background checks. Tips and forms are provided to help you reach a selection decision, as well as to do the actual hiring and orienting of the new hire.

It is hoped that this book will provide a framework for you to develop a successful staffing program.

ONE

Background

1

The Labor Market

It is a well-known fact that foodservices are having problems getting qualified employees. "Help Wanted" signs seem to be everywhere, from traditional newspaper advertisements to, more recently, cash register receipts. Not only are there fewer applicants responding to these signs, but also the country's labor force is undergoing significant demographic changes. For the first time, white males are in the minority in the labor force, making up only 46 percent of the work force (Copeland, 1988). This trend will continue due to the combination of a declining and older white American population and a younger, growing minority population. Both minorities and women will be entering the work force in large numbers.

So who is the typical nonsupervisory foodservice employee? A profile follows (National Restaurant Association, 1990):

- Female (60 percent)
- White
- Under 30 years of age (58 percent)
- High school graduate (62 percent)
- Unmarried (63 percent)
- Lives with relatives (81 percent)
- Lives in a household with an average U.S. income
- Works part-time, averaging 26 hours a week
- Has been working in the current position for less than one year (40 percent)

3

When compared to other industries, foodservice employees are more likely to be female, younger, and unmarried, and less likely to have a high school diploma. Foodservice employees are similar in race and ethnic origin to employees in other industries.

In this chapter we will look first at why we have a labor shortage, and then we will discuss in more detail the present labor situation and responses to it. Lastly, the problem of literacy among today's applicants and employees will be discussed.

Reasons for the Labor Shortage

There are many reasons for the labor shortage. To begin with, the number of young people, who represent an important segment of the foodservice work force, has been on the decline since the post-World War II "baby boom" ended in the mid-1960s. The "baby boom" was followed by a "baby bust." The "baby bust" generation, born between 1965 and 1979, was much smaller in number. The Bureau of Labor Statistics projects that the teenage labor force will shrink until 1992. After 1992, foodservice operators should start to see more teenage applicants as children of the "baby boom" generation reach working age. The number of young adults from the ages of 20 to 21 will start to rise in 1995, and the number of young adults from the ages of 22 to 24 will start to rise modestly in 1998 (Michalski, 1990).

The drop in the number of teenagers has occurred at a time when the foodservice industry is growing and continues to have more jobs that need to be filled. Between 1988 and 2000, the Bureau of Labor Statistics projects 2 million additional jobs in foodservice. By the year 2000, the foodservice industry will employ approximately 10.7 million workers, the largest number of jobs for any industry. This rate of growth is higher than for the total U.S. labor force (Michalski, 1990).

In addition, there has been much competition for the 16 to 24 age group from retail and other industries, and also high employee turnover rates. The high yearly turnover rate makes the labor shortage even worse because of the increased frequency of having to find replacements. *Turnover* refers to the loss of an employee who must be replaced. Turnover, defined as a percentage, is calculated as follows:

$$\text{Turnover Rate} = \frac{\text{Number of Replacements}}{\text{Average Number of Employees}} \times 100\%$$

In the restaurant business, about half of all separations—such as resignation or termination—occur within the first 30 days (Carlino, 1988). Turnover rates for various types of foodservices vary, but many fall between 200 and 250 percent. In other words, an operator can count on replacing each of his or her current employees at least twice during a 12-month period of time.

Turnover can occur due to either voluntary or involuntary reasons. Voluntary reasons for leaving a job include resignation, retirement, or transfer. Involuntary reasons include being terminated, laid off, or discharged, such as when a temporary position ends. Causes of turnover may include poor employee selection, wages that are not competitive, few opportunities for advancement, inadequate orientation and training, poor supervision, and an unfavorable working environment.

Finally, another reason for the labor shortage is the negative view some people have of working in foodservice. This image may come, in part, from the fact that the average wages paid, $4.35 excluding tips in 1986, are significantly below the average hourly rate for nonsupervisory jobs, $8.76 (National Restaurant Association, 1988). Foodservice wages have been increasing since 1986.

The Labor Situation

A survey done by the Gallup Organization for the National Restaurant Association in December 1989 reported the following labor shortage problems cited by foodservice managers:

- Fewer qualified job applicants (45 percent)
- Fewer applicants for jobs paid on an hourly basis (43 percent)
- Increased turnover (32 percent)
- Fewer applicants for salaried jobs (30 percent)

Whereas these problems were previously more confined to the East, other parts of the United States are experiencing them as well. The positions reported as the hardest to fill are cooks, servers, and dishwashers.

In general, chain and franchise foodservice operators have more labor shortage problems than independents. The 1989 National Restaurant Association survey showed that chain and franchise operators report more problems with turnover and fewer applicants for jobs.

According to the Bureau of Labor Statistics, the jobs which are expected to show the highest rate of growth between 1988 and 2000 are

Bread and pastry bakers
Hosts and hostesses
Servers
Server assistants
Restaurant cooks and chefs
All other foodservice workers, such as dishwashers
Food preparation workers, except fast-food workers
Bartenders

Fast-food jobs will show the slowest growth, yet, by the year 2000, three out of every ten people employed in foodservice will be working in fast food (Michalski, 1990).

Responses to the Labor Shortage

In the same survey done by the Gallup Organization for the National Restaurant Association in December 1989, foodservice managers reported that they were taking the following steps, or were expecting to do so, to manage the labor shortage:

Improve training (73 percent)
Increase starting wages (61 percent)
Improve benefits (46 percent)
Increase hours worked for hourly employees (39 percent)
Expand recruiting efforts (38 percent)
Install labor-saving equipment (35 percent)

The first four steps are discussed in detail in Chapter 4, "Introduction to Recruiting," and new sources of employees, such as the handicapped, older workers, and immigrants, are discussed in more detail in Chapter 6, "External Recruiting."

Examples of labor-saving equipment include dishwashers, cooking and food preparation equipment, and computer equipment. In addition, managers report using labor-saving techniques, such as on-going employee training, better scheduling, and developing more efficient work areas.

Operators are also using current and past employees to meet staffing needs better. This includes using part-timers, doing cross-training, and having a temporary employee pool, which include former employees.

Foodservice is marked by frantic periods followed by lulls, during which productivity is usually low. Part-time employees give more flexibility in terms of scheduling during those peak periods, which means that there will be fewer employees hanging around when business is slow. They also receive fewer (or no) benefits than full-timers and rarely receive overtime pay. However, when part-timers who really want full-time hours are hired, it should not be surprising if they leave soon after being hired. Hiring part-timers who constantly ask to work more hours and eventually leave because they do not get enough hours is not desirable. On the other hand, hiring someone who really wants part-time hours, such as a mother with school-age children, is more advantageous. Data from the Bureau of Labor Statistics show that the use of part-time employees may be slowing in foodservice.

In addition to hiring part-time hourly employees, it is possible to hire part-time professionals, such as human resource managers or marketing directors. This may be convenient, of course, for smaller businesses that do not need someone full-time to do these or other professional functions. The benefits to the business include salary savings and reduced benefits costs, as well as convenience. In addition, part-time professionals tend to use their time more wisely and to take care of personal matters on their own time instead of on company time.

Cross-training of employees has proved to be most effective in dealing with sick calls and time off, such as vacations. Without cross-training, a larger staff may be needed in order to respond to paid and unpaid time off. For instance, in many fast-food restaurants, employees are trained to be crew members and can work in many different positions.

Some operators have experimented with an in-house temporary employee pool. This pool may include retirees or other former employees who are familiar with foodservice jobs. Temporary employees can be scheduled to work as needed to cover vacant job positions or an employee who is out, or to help out during a seasonal busy period. Temporary employees are advantageous to the employer because they typically receive no benefits and cannot file for unemployment insurance or wrongful discharge.

The Future Labor Force

Table 1-1 shows some interesting statistics regarding the future makeup of the U.S. work force. The average age of the work force is rising and, by the year 2000, over 50 percent will be middle-aged (between 35 to 54 years of age). The average worker will be 39 years old. The number of senior citizens will continue to increase, and they

Table 1-1   Labor Force in the Year 2000

(Civilian labor force aged 16 and older—including employed workers and unemployed actively seeking work—in the year 2000; numbers in thousands)

	Number in Labor Force	Percent of Work Force	Percent Change in Labor Force 1988–2000
Men (16 and older)			
Total	74,324	52.7%	11.1%
16 to 24	11,352	8.1	−3.4
25 to 34	16,572	11.8	−16.1
35 to 44	20,188	14.3	25.6
45 to 54	16,395	14.6	55.2
55 to 64	7,796	5.5	14.1
65 and older	2,021	1.4	3.1
Women (16 and older)			
Total	66,810	47.3%	22.0%
16 to 24	11,104	7.9	3.0
25 to 34	15,105	10.7	−4.2
35 to 44	18,584	13.2	39.1
45 to 54	14,423	10.2	68.9
55 to 64	6,140	4.3	23.4
65 and older	1,454	1.0	9.8
White			
Total	118,981	84.3%	13.6%
Men	63,288	44.8	8.5
Women	55,693	39.5	19.9
Black			
Total	16,465	11.7%	24.7%
Men	8,007	5.7	21.4
Women	8,458	6.0	28.0
Other			
Total	5,688	4.0%	53.4%

Source: Bureau of Labor Statistics, 1989/*American Demographics Magazine,* March 1990.

will continue to fill some of the gaps left by the shrinking number of younger workers in foodservices. Some foodservice operators, such as McDonalds, have recruiting programs designed to bring in senior citizens.

The vast majority of new workers entering the work force through the 1990s will be women, minorities, and immigrants (Hopkins,

Nestleroth, and Bolick, 1991). By 2000, 47 percent of the work force will be women. Not only are more women working, but more mothers are working as well. Over half the mothers of children under 6 years of age work outside the home.

Minority groups will comprise 29 percent of all new workers entering the labor force. About one-third of these new workers will be black, with Hispanics also contributing significantly. The populations of blacks and Hispanics have been growing because of both birth rates and immigration (especially for Hispanics). Although many minority job applicants are well educated and trained, some are economically and socially disadvantaged and employers will have to help them enter the work force.

The United States is experiencing its Fourth Wave of immigration which started in the 1960s. Immigrants come primarily from Latin America and Asia, although significant numbers still come from Europe, the Caribbean, and the Middle East. Immigrants arrive with a wide range of educational and social backgrounds. Many are not familiar with English, and those from areas such as Latin America and Asia are often economically and socially disadvantaged. However, most immigrants want very much to improve their lives and try very hard.

The Literacy Problem

If we use a strict definition, *literacy* means the ability to read and write. In its broader definition, it is used interchangeably with the term "basic skills," which includes reading, writing, basic arithmetic, oral communication, and the ability to speak English. To what extent an individual possesses these skills and is considered literate varies among different cultures and at different times. For example, the requirements for literacy in the United States were actually lower 30 years ago than they are now. This is due in part to the fact that reading is now a requirement of almost every job every day.

Illiteracy is a growing concern in the foodservice business for many reasons.

- It reduces the number of qualified applicants available for jobs.
- It contributes to accidents on the job, low productivity, errors, absenteeism, and lost management time.
- It prevents employees from being promoted.
- It will require time and other resources to overcome.

The number of literacy programs for employees, although few, are growing in number. There are basically two types of literacy programs: general literacy programs and job-related basic skills training. General literacy programs include instruction in basic skills and often work toward the earning of a high school diploma or equivalent. A job-related program is designed to teach employees basic skills so that they can become more proficient on the job and also more promotable. The content of the program, as well as the approach, are determined by the nature of the job. This type of program is more likely to meet the needs both of employees and employers. Employees frequently have more pride in themselves and in their work after attending such a program, resulting in improved job performance and morale as well as making them more promotable.

In a survey of organizations providing remedial training in the workplace done by *Training* magazine (Lee, 1989), it was found that basic math, reading, and writing were offered by over 40 percent of responding companies. English as a second language was offered by almost 33 percent, and other subjects (primarily for a High School Equivalency Diploma) were offered by 17 percent. This survey also looked at how much companies spend for this training. Although cost estimates varied tremendously, companies that used public education programs spent very little in direct costs. For two dozen companies that developed and implemented their own programs, the average cost was $200 per person.

The following are steps to use when developing and implementing a job-related basic skills program.

1. Assess needs and resources.
2. Create a planning team.
3. Select an educational provider organization.
4. Develop instructional objectives, curriculum, instructional methods, and teaching aids.
5. Find a classroom.
6. Staff the program.
7. Recruit employees.
8. Monitor the program.

Initially, a company needs to assess both its needs for a program and the resources to provide one if needed. The following questions can help.

What skills are needed to perform the various jobs?

How many employees are having problems doing their jobs due to a lack of basic skills?

Within which job categories are these problems most frequently occurring?

Are there enough employees with poor job skills to warrant a job-related basic skills program?

Are any changes expected in employees' jobs that would require more skills which some of the current employees could not handle?

Does the company have someone who can oversee the development, implementation, and monitoring of a program?

Is there room on-site for such a program, or will it have to be held off-site?

Will employees be paid while they attend the basic skills program?

If employees spend part of their work time attending classes, how will this affect the operation of the company?

How much money is available for such a program?

A valuable resource in doing the needs assessment is your job description file. Knowing the basic skills competencies required for the various jobs will make it easier to determine your needs.

Although one individual can oversee the development of a basic skills program, better results are achieved when a planning team is involved. Members of this planning team may include foodservice managers and supervisors, employees, human resource and training personnel, and union representatives.

Because most companies do not have the ability to develop their own basic skills program, they select an educational provider organization best suited to their needs. Here are some suggestions:

Your local school district, which may administer an adult basic education program.

The adult and continuing education unit of your state education department.

Colleges and universities in your area, many of which operate adult basic education programs, some having special expertise in job-related skills programs.

Nonprofit literacy groups such as Laubach Literacy and Literacy Volunteers of America which are the two major voluntary organizations. Both have state and local affiliate operations around the country. These affiliate units recruit, train, and support volunteer tutors who give one-on-one and small group instruction in various settings. Community-based organizations are another potential source of help. These highly localized entities operate under various names and can best be found by contacting state or local literacy planning bodies or the Association for Community Based Education in Washington, D.C. They have an especially good track record with adults at the lowest educational level.

For-profit organizations and individuals can also provide job-related basic skills training. The Business Council for Effective Literacy can provide leads in this area. Those charged with state-wide planning in your state should be able to help as well.

Private Industry Councils are actively involved in this area in many states and localities. Many use funds from the Job Training Partnership Act to develop cooperative job-related basic skills programs.

Your local library and/or State Library Office are also resources. (Business Council for Effective Literacy, 1987)

Selecting a provider is the most important decision in this process and should therefore be done with the most care.

What kind of past experience has the provider organization had in working in a foodservice setting?

What kind of past experience has it had in doing programs for your particular population group(s)?

Is its philosophy of adult education similar to yours?

What will it do for a needs assessment?

What will the components of the program be? Does the provider organization meet your needs? To what extent will it customize the program to your jobs and make the program job-related? What will the employees be able to do after they have finished the program?

Does the length of the program meet your needs?

How will instructors be selected and trained? What are the qualifications and experience of the instructors? How will they be supervised? Do they receive any staff development?

What will you have to provide?

Who will be the primary contact person, and will this person work well with you?

How will the provider organization evaluate how well the program is going?

A final question to ask is whether this particular provider can actually accomplish what is wanted, within a reasonable time frame.

Once a provider has been selected, you will need to work together on developing instructional objectives (what results you want from the training), curriculum (what to teach), instructional methods (how to teach it), and teaching aids. You will also need to decide when classes will meet. Whatever is taught, the following principles should be incorporated into the program.

- Employees' prior knowledge about a job content area should be acknowledged and built upon in designing teaching materials and approaches.
- Materials actually used in specific jobs should be used extensively as instructional resources.
- Trainees should spend time actually reading and writing about the content area they are studying.
- Teachers should be creative in how they present information about a content area.
- Teach reading strategies appropriate to varied on-the-job reading tasks. (Business Council for Effective Literacy, 1987)

Next, a classroom site needs to be located. This is an important decision, because employees will interpret an inviting learning environment as meaning that management thinks the program is important. Also, an appropriate classroom site may motivate employees. Features of a good classroom include being attractive, comfortable, roomy, quiet, well lit, convenient to get to, flexible for both group and individual study, equipped with appropriate furniture and storage and display spaces, and permanent.

Regarding staffing of the new program, a program coordinator who will be the main liaison with the program and who will be responsible for monitoring the program and the provider's performance needs to be found. This person must have good communication skills and be quite familiar with the program objectives. He or she also will have to support the educational provider organization as needed.

The provider organization will provide a program director who should be experienced in implementing and running a job-related basic skills program, including curriculum and instructional methods development, learner assessment, teacher training and supervision, and record maintenance. Any teachers within the program should be knowledgeable about, and experienced in, teaching adult learners job-related basic skills. Teachers also need to be sensitive to the needs of the adult learners and to be flexible with teaching approaches and job-related teaching materials. If properly supervised and trained, volunteers can supplement the instruction given by teachers and provide the individualized attention many employees need.

The next job is to recruit employees for training. This can be a very sensitive issue, so it must be handled carefully and respectfully.

- Do not call the program "Remedial Training" or anything that will make the employee feel even more inadequate. Instead, use upbeat names, such as "Career Development," so that employees will feel it is a positive step, which of course it is!
- Make sure employees are told that the program is being offered to help them function on the job, not as a way to terminate them. Explain that management does care and value them enough as employees to help them.
- Provide on-site instruction whenever possible to avoid employees wasting their time and money going elsewhere. If instruction must take place off-site, such as at a library, offer to reimburse employees for transportation costs.
- Provide incentives for participation, such as pay at their normal hourly rate, while they are attending the program. Without being paid, most employees will find other things to do which are more important to them.

The following are various recruiting methods which can be used:

Word of mouth through managers, supervisors, and employees
Announcement of the program at a meeting
Posters and notices
Articles in newsletters
Notices sent to employees' homes or put in their paychecks (Do not use pink paper!)

Once the employees have started attending the program, the program coordinator needs to monitor the program to determine if program instruction and operation are working well on a day-to-day basis. The program coordinator also needs to monitor the evaluation results provided by the educational provider organization to determine if the performance goals are being met.

In conclusion, basic skills training programs which have the best attendance, highest retention of employees, and greatest achievements are those that

Are specifically job-related
Are taught by well-trained teachers

Use appropriate curriculum and materials
Are offered on company time (Business Council for Effective Literacy, 1987)

The following is an example of a literacy program in a foodservice.*
The appendix contains resources for developing a literacy program.

Carmen's Pizzeria is typical of the small businesses served by the 12-year-old GRASP Adult Learning Center in Illinois. Started with federal funding, now sustained by state and local funds, GRASP offers basic skills, English as a Second Language, and high school equivalency courses, working under contract with small businesses in the Chicago area (the majority of which need ESL instruction for their employees). The curriculum is customized to each particular job setting. The charge to the business is $35 per employee for the first 10-week course and $40 per hour for each 10-week course thereafter. Carmen's 20 employees are from Mexico and South American and have little or no English proficiency. A GRASP teacher arrives at the restaurant four days a week and works with the employees on their language skills from 2:00 to 4:00 P.M. The owner of the pizzeria is convinced that the program cost is a small price to pay for cooks that can better understand special orders, waitresses who communicate better with the public, and increased confidence and morale among all the staff. Attendance is reportedly 100 percent and employees even come on their days off.

*Source: Business Council for Effective Literary. 1987. Job-related basic skills. *Business Council for Effective Literacy Bulletin* 1(2):11 – 12.

2

Job Descriptions

Before I explain how to write job descriptions, common definitions for "job," "position," and other terms must be discussed.

Definitions

A job consists of related activities and duties, performed on a regular basis for a set compensation. Jobs provide the basis for forming work groups or crews, departments, and larger units for achieving the organization's objectives. Jobs in a foodservice may include server, cook, and manager.

A position consists of duties and responsibilities performed by only one employee. For example, in a restaurant there are three cook positions occupied by three employees, but all of them have only one job (cook). An occupation is a group of similar jobs found in different companies. Lastly, a career is a sequence of occupations, jobs, and positions that a person has during his or her working life.

Position: A given individual performing one or more duties
Job: A group of positions with the same or similar activities and duties
Occupation: A group of similar jobs found in different organizations
Career: A sequence of occupations, jobs, and positions a person occupies during his or her working life

Job Description: A description of the job as a whole, as it relates to the what, how, why, and where of a job; may also include job requirements

Position Description: Daily work assignment for a position

Duty: A segment of work activity comprised of one task or several related tasks with an identifiable output; for example, a cook prepares breakfast

Task: A distinct work activity with a specific function, for example, making change

Responsibility: A description of results expected or of how an employee is accountable for something delegated to him or her

Job descriptions explain the what, how, why, and where of a job, and may include job qualifications. They therefore provide needed information for recruiting and selecting employees. This chapter will help you develop job descriptions for your operation.

Uses of Job Descriptions

There are dozens of ways to use job descriptions, although most organizations use them in only five or six problem areas. Job descriptions probably have the potential of being the most powerful management tool of all. One reason they are not used more often is that they are often poorly prepared. However, when they are well done, they are invaluable in manpower planning, recruiting, interviewing and evaluating applicants, final selection, and training. In addition to being used in staffing, they can be used to

Make clear to both management and employees exactly who does what and what is expected

Assign work

Evaluate work

Take disciplinary action

Serve as a foundation for performance evaluation

Permit accurate and defensible assignments of job and pay levels, thereby supporting job evaluation systems

Determine training and development needs

Help in career guidance

Provide the information needed for reporting in compliance with the Equal Employment Opportunity requirements

Help the new manager, who needs to learn who does what
Spot areas of work overlap or duplication, or to prepare work studies in order to design improvements

As you can see, once developed, job descriptions can be very useful for many different individuals.

Writing Job Descriptions

There is some disagreement as to what a job description should include but widespread agreement as to what it should not include. A job description should not refer to the person doing the job, since it refers to a job, not a person. In addition, a description of when tasks are to be accomplished, such as the time of day when the tabletops are to be cleaned and sanitized, should be put into a position description, as seen in Table 2-1.

A job description has six sections:

1. Job identification
2. A job summary
3. A list of results and duties
4. The job setting
5. Job qualifications
6. The signature of the person approving the job description and the approval date

Although qualifications may sometimes appear in a separate document, referred to as a "job specification," you may want to keep all this information together. Figures 2-1, 2-2, 2-3, 2-4, 2-5, and 2-6 show job descriptions for a host/hostess, a server, a dining room attendant, a chef, a cook, and a storekeeper.

JOB IDENTIFICATION

Job identification includes the job title, such as cook, which needs to be descriptive of the work to be done and, when possible, the level within the organization. For example, the title "head cook" may involve some supervision and may be at a higher level in the organization. Job titles should not include the word *man* or *woman*. In addition to job title, this section may also include the following:

Table 2-1 Sample Position Description

WORK SCHEDULE

Position Title: <u>Baker</u>   Shift: <u>5:30 A.M. to 2:00 P.M.</u>
Effective Date: <u>1/90</u>

Time	Duties
5:30 A.M.	Report to work in uniform and punch in
5:30–6:00 A.M.	Check production sheets for baking needs; prepare area for production; gather ingredients
6:00–9:00 A.M.	Bake all goods in a timely manner according to production sheets; keep work area as clean as possible
9:00–9:15 A.M.	Break
9:15–1:00 P.M.	Continue producing all needed items and keep area clean
1:00–1:30 P.M.	Lunch break
1:30–2:30 P.M.	Put away all ingredients and baked goods; clean and sanitize table tops
2:30 P.M.	Punch out

The department name
Grade level
Location of the job
Whether job is exempt or nonexempt
Hours of the job
The reporting relationship (superiors and subordinates)

An exempt job is exempt from federal minimum wage and overtime pay requirements. Both exempt and nonexempt jobs are discussed in more detail in Chapter 3.

JOB SUMMARY

A job summary should consist of only one or two sentences and should explain concisely the what and why of the job. It need not go

Fig. 2-1   JOB DESCRIPTION—HOST/HOSTESS

JOB DESCRIPTION

JOB IDENTIFICATION
Job Title: __Host/Hostess__
Department: __Dining Room__   Reports to: __Dining Room Manager__
Hours: __10:30 A.M.—7:00 P.M.; 2:00—10:30 P.M.__
Exempt or Nonexempt: __Exempt__
Grade: __10__

JOB SUMMARY
Assures consistently the satisfaction and dining pleasure of all guests

RESULTS AND DUTIES
1. Manages dining room operation so as to ensure guest satisfaction
   a. Takes reservations according to policy
   b. Conducts daily lineups of staff
   c. Greets guests at the door and seats them according to standard
   d. Observes and directs service of guests by staff to make sure service standards are being met
   e. Handles guest complaints according to policy
   f. Checks on the responsible service of alcohol by servers

2. Manages human resources to ensure satisfactory employee job performance
   a. Interviews and hires staff
   b. Orients and trains new employees using training procedures
   c. Disciplines staff according to policy and in consultation with Dining Room Manager
   d. Calculates payroll hours for staff
   e. Schedules staff

Fig. 2-1 Continued

f. Coaches staff on daily basis

g. Formally evaluates staff twice a year

h. Revises job descriptions yearly

i. Holds weekly meetings with staff to give information, to build teamwork, and to discuss concerns

3. Maintains dining room so it is kept clean, in good repair, and fully stocked with supplies to ensure guest satisfaction and safety

a. Checks on completion of sidework

b. Speaks with Dining Room Manager on any repairs needed

c. Gives orders for dining room supplies to Dining Room Manager

4. Keeps costs under control

a. Assists in planning dining room budget for personnel and supplies

b. Keeps dining room payroll and supplies within the budgeted allowance

JOB SETTING

Contacts: Guests, dining room staff, managers

Working Conditions: Works in temperature-controlled dining room and service area, which become congested during busy times

Physical Demands: Is standing and walking most of time; does some lifting

Work Hazards: Hot surfaces, steam, wet floors, some heavy lifting

Fig. 2-1 Continued

JOB QUALIFICATIONS

Knowledge: Must have basic knowledge of food, wines, liquors, cooking, and American-style service; must be familiar with basic supervisory practices

Skills and Abilities: Supervises personnel fairly; deals with guests and handles complaints and problems efficiently and courteously; controls costs; presents a neat and well-groomed appearance; orders supplies; handles cash; is honest; handles stress; works hard; solves problems; is reliable; works as a team member

Work Experience: One year satisfactory experience as a server required; additional one year satisfactory experience as host/hostess preferred

Education and Training: Service or supervisory training, or both, preferred

Incumbent Signature: _____ Date: _____

Approval Signature: _____ Date: _____

Approval Signature: _____ Date: _____

Fig. 2-2 JOB DESCRIPTION—SERVER

JOB DESCRIPTION

JOB IDENTIFICATION
Job Title: Server
Department: Dining Room   Reports to: Dining Room Manager
Hours: 10:30 A.M.–2:30 P.M.; 2:30–6:30 P.M.; 4:30–10:30 P.M.
Exempt or Nonexempt: Nonexempt
Grade: 6

JOB SUMMARY
Serves guests in a courteous, helpful, and prompt manner

RESULTS AND DUTIES
1. Serves guests and meets their needs to ensure a
   pleasant dining experience and a return visit
   a. Accurately describes all menu items and wines
      available; names brand names of liquors available
   b. Sets up table and station according to standards
   c. Greets guests promptly and courteously
   d. Serves guests according to service standards
   e. Follows guest relations policy
   f. Performs closing duties and sidework

2. Handles cash and credit cards properly
   a. Fills out guest check according to policy
   b. Accepts and processes guest payments per policy

3. Serves alcohol responsibly to prevent accidents and
   possible lawsuits
   a. Serves alcohol according to policy

4. Works as a team member to maintain a pleasant work
   environment
   a. Comes to work on time
   b. Is not absent from work excessively

Fig. 2-2   Continued

   c. Reports to work dressed according to the dress code
   d. Maintains sanitation and safety standards
   e. Performs other duties as requested

JOB SETTING
Contacts: Guests, dining room personnel, cooking staff

Working Conditions: Works in temperature-controlled dining room and service area, which become congested during busy times

Physical Demands: Is standing and walking most of time; frequently lifts heavy trays

Work Hazards: Hot surfaces, steam, wet floors, heavy lifting, sharp knives

JOB QUALIFICATIONS
Knowledge: Must have basic knowledge of food and cooking

Skills and Abilities: Presents a good appearance; is neat and well groomed; interacts with guests in a courteous and helpful manner; works well with other personnel; writes neatly; performs basic mathematical functions (addition, subtraction, multiplication, and division); sets tables, serves and clears; is honest; handles stress; works hard; is reliable

Work Experience: Six months satisfactory experience as a server required; one year preferred

Education and Training: High school diploma or service training, or both, preferred

Incumbent Signature: _____ Date: _____
Approval Signature: _____ Date: _____
Approval Signature: _____ Date: _____

Fig. 2-3 JOB DESCRIPTION—DINING ROOM ATTENDANT

JOB DESCRIPTION

JOB IDENTIFICATION
Job Title: _Dining Room Attendant_
Department: _Dining Room_   Reports to: _Host/Hostess_
Hours: _10:30 A.M.—2:30 P.M.; 2:30—6:30 P.M.; 6:30—10:30 P.M._
Exempt or Nonexempt: _Nonexempt_
Grade: _5_

JOB SUMMARY
Assists servers in providing courteous and prompt service to guests

RESULTS AND DUTIES
1. Assists servers to provide quality service
   a. Removes used dishes, silverware, linen, and ashtrays according to service standards
   b. Resets tables as needed
   c. Refills guests' butter, other condiments, water glasses, and other beverages as needed
   d. Performs assigned sidework

2. Works as a team member to maintain a pleasant work environment
   a. Comes to work on time
   b. Is not absent from work excessively
   c. Reports to work dressed according to the dress code
   d. Maintains sanitation and safety standards
   e. Performs other duties as requested

JOB SETTING
Contacts: _Dining room personnel, host/hostess, dishwasher_

Working Conditions: _Works in temperature-controlled dining room and service area, which become congested during busy times_

Fig. 2-3 Continued

Physical Demands: Is standing and walking most of time; frequently lifts heavy trays

Work Hazards: Hot surfaces, steam, wet floors, heavy lifting

JOB QUALIFICATIONS

Knowledge: No specific knowledge required; entry-level position

Skills and Abilities: Presents a good appearance; is neat and well groomed; interacts with dining room personnel in a courteous and helpful manner; is observant and reacts quickly, accepts and follows directions, and works calmly with minimal disruption to guests; works hard; is reliable

Work Experience: Six months satisfactory experience as a server required; one year preferred

Education and Training: None required; entry-level position

Incumbent Signature: _____ Date: _____
Approval Signature: _____ Date: _____
Approval Signature: _____ Date: _____

Fig. 2-4   JOB DESCRIPTION—CHEF

JOB DESCRIPTION

JOB IDENTIFICATION

Job Title: _Chef_____

Department: _Kitchen_____   Reports to: _General Manager_____

Hours: _11:00 P.M.—8:00 P.M._____

Exempt or Nonexempt: _Exempt_____

Grade: _11_____

JOB SUMMARY

Provides high—quality food for guests

RESULTS AND DUTIES

1. Serves well—prepared foods in a safe manner
   a. Supervises cooking staff in the production of all
      menu items, including using and adjusting recipes,
      using high—quality ingredients, operating kitchen
      equipment, evaluating foods, portioning, and
      garnishing
   b. Supervises safe handling of food
   c. Purchases food, beverages, and supplies
   d. Supervises receiving and storage of all food and
      beverages to ensure they are adequate and of high
      quality
   e. Supervises weekly physical inventory

2. Keeps kitchen clean to pass inspections and keeps
   equipment in working order to prevent equipment
   failure
   a. Supervises sanitation staff
   b. Keeps up preventative maintenance program for
      kitchen equipment
   c. Gets equipment fixed as needed

Fig. 2-4 Continued

3. Keeps costs within budget
    a. Assists in planning food and labor budget
    b. Controls food and supply waste and theft
    c. Keeps overtime pay within constraints

4. Manages human resources to ensure satisfactory
   employee job performance
    a. Interviews and hires staff
    b. Orients and trains new employees using training
       procedures
    c. Disciplines staff according to policy in
       consultation with General Manager
    d. Calculates payroll hours for staff
    e. Schedules staff
    f. Coaches staff on daily basis
    g. Formally evaluates staff twice a year
    h. Revises job descriptions yearly
    i. Holds weekly meetings with staff to give
       information, to build teamwork, and to discuss
       concerns

JOB SETTING

Contacts: Other cooking staff, chef, servers, cleaning
crew, storekeeper

Working Conditions: Works in hot area with much humidity at
times; area becomes congested and noisy during busy times

Physical Demands: Is standing most of time; does much
walking; frequently does heavy lifting

Work Hazards: Hot surfaces, steam, wet floors, hot grease,
heavy lifting, knives and other sharp objects, electrical
shocks

Fig. 2-4 Continued

JOB QUALIFICATIONS

Knowledge: Must have knowledge of American-style cooking and basic supervisory practices; qualities of foods, beverages, and supplies; health department regulations

Skills and Abilities: Measures; uses a knife; identifies and uses various pieces of small and large kitchen equipment; reads and follows recipes; does basic math (addition, subtraction, multiplication, and division); uses any cooking method; determines degree of doneness in cooked foods; uses portion control tools; garnishes; works well with others; supervises consistently and fairly; purchases and receives foods, beverages, and supplies; does physical inventory; maintains a clean kitchen according to health regulations; is honest; handles stress; works hard; solves problems; is reliable

Work Experience: One year of satisfactory experience as a chef required supervising at least four employees

Education and Training: One year culinary training required

Incumbent Signature: _____ Date: _____
Approval Signature: _____ Date: _____
Approval Signature: _____ Date: _____

Fig. 2-5 JOB DESCRIPTION—COOK

JOB DESCRIPTION

JOB IDENTIFICATION
Job Title: Cook
Department: Kitchen   Reports to: Chef
Hours: 9:00 A.M.—5:00 P.M. or 2:00 P.M.—10:00 P.M.
Exempt or Nonexempt: Nonexempt
Grade: 8

JOB SUMMARY
Prepares all menu items to facility standards and in a
timely manner   ▶

RESULTS AND DUTIES
1. Prepares tasty foods for guests under the guidance of
    the Chef
    a. Uses and follows recipes
    b. Adjusts recipes accurately
    c. Uses high-quality ingredients and measures them
        accurately
    d. Operates all kitchen equipment correctly
    e. Taste tests and evaluates foods before serving to
        make sure standards are met; consults with Chef if
        has any concerns
    f. Portions food into standard portions
    g. Garnishes food in appealing manner

2. Uses and maintains production records to prevent waste
    a. Uses and follows production sheets
    b. Keeps written records of all food produced
    c. Keeps written records of all foods left over

Fig. 2-5 Continued

3. Serves food that is safe to eat
   a. Follows facility's safe food—handling guidelines.
   b. Cleans and sanitizes work area according to cleaning schedule

4. Works as a team member to maintain pleasant work environment
   a. Comes to work on time
   b. Is not absent from work excessively
   c. Reports to work dressed according to the dress code
   d. Performs other duties as requested

JOB SETTING

Contacts: Other cooking staff, chef, servers, cleaning crew, storekeeper

Working Conditions: Works in hot area with much humidity at times; area becomes congested and noisy during busy times

Physical Demands: Is standing most of time; does much walking; frequently does heavy lifting

Work Hazards: Hot surfaces, steam, wet floors, hot grease, heavy lifting, knives and other sharp objects, electrical shocks

Fig. 2-5 Continued

JOB QUALIFICATIONS

Knowledge: Cooking terminology and ingredients

Skills and Abilities: Measures; uses a knife; identifies and uses various pieces of small and large kitchen equipment; reads and follows recipes; does basic math (addition, subtraction, multiplication, and division); uses any cooking method; determines degree of doneness in cooked foods; uses portion control tools; garnishes; works well with others; dresses per policy; is honest; handles stress; works hard; is reliable

Work Experience: One year of satisfactory experience as a cook required; two to three years cooking experience preparing a variety of menu items preferred

Education and Training: Culinary training preferred

Incumbent Signature: _____ Date: _____
Approval Signature: _____ Date: _____
Approval Signature: _____ Date: _____

Fig. 2-6 JOB DESCRIPTION—STOREKEEPER

JOB DESCRIPTION

JOB IDENTIFICATION

Job Title: Storekeeper

Department: Kitchen   Reports to: Chef

Hours: 8:00 A.M.—4:30 P.M. Monday to Friday

Exempt or Nonexempt: Nonexempt

Grade: 8

JOB SUMMARY

Receives, stores, issues, and inventories food, beverages, disposables, and equipment used by kitchen staff

RESULTS AND DUTIES

1. Receives all incoming goods to ensure adequate and high-quality stock
   a. Verifies actual quantity received against vendor's invoice and purchase order
   b. Checks price on vendor's invoice against purchase order price
   c. Checks quality of incoming stock according to policy and procedure
   d. Speaks with Chef if there are any discrepancies or poor quality

2. Stores all incoming stock to maintain quality and food safety
   a. Unpacks stock and removes cardboard boxes to disposal area to decrease pest problems
   b. Stores refrigerated and frozen foods within 30 minutes of arrival to decrease food safety problems
   c. Rotates stock, using the first-in, first-out principle to ensure fresh products

---

Fig. 2-6 **Continued**

3. Maintains records of stock, to permit accurate food costing and purchasing
   a. Issues stock during posted hours, using stock requisition forms, according to policy and procedure
   b. Takes physical inventory on weekly basis, using inventory book

4. Keeps storage areas clean to ensure a safe product
   a. Cleans and maintains all storage areas according to posted cleaning schedule

5. Works as a team member to maintain a pleasant work environment
   a. Comes to work on time
   b. Is not absent from work excessively
   c. Reports to work dressed according to the dress code
   d. Maintains safety standards
   e. Performs other duties as requested

JOB SETTING

Contacts: Vendor's drivers, kitchen staff

Working Conditions: Works in cold freezers and refrigerators and outdoors, where temperatures vary; areas become cramped at times

Physical Demands: Is standing most of time; does much walking; frequently does heavy lifting

Work Hazards: Back injuries due to lifting

Fig. 2-6 Continued

JOB QUALIFICATIONS

Knowledge: Must have basic knowledge of foods

Skills and Abilities: Performs basic mathematical calculations (addition, subtraction, multiplication, and division); counts accurately; performs heavy physical work, including lifting up to 80 pounds; follows oral and written instructions; works with minimal supervision; must be able to work well with others, due to frequent contacts with drivers and kitchen staff; dresses per policy; is honest; handles stress; works hard; is reliable

Work Experience: One year satisfactory experience as storekeeper preferred

Education and Training: High school graduate or storekeeper training, or both, preferred

Incumbent Signature: _____ Date: _____
Approval Signature: _____ Date: _____
Approval Signature: _____ Date: _____

into specific tasks, simply the major or overall duty and purpose of the job.

RESULTS AND DUTIES

Next there should be a list of results and duties. Duties are segments of work activities consisting of specified tasks. For example, a cashier's duty is to handle cash sales. Tasks involved in this duty include ringing up sales and making change correctly. The appendix lists duties for many foodservice jobs.

Job descriptions have traditionally listed statements of job duties without giving any explanation of why they are done. By writing the results of various job duties, the person holding the job will see why those duties are important and how they relate to the overall operation. For instance, a duty-oriented statement for a host/hostess may note, "Greets customers courteously." This could be made results-oriented by noting, "Makes customers feel welcome and comfortable by greeting them courteously within one minute of arrival." When many duties are done to accomplish one result, the result can be stated first, and then the duties used to achieve it can be listed under it as seen in Figs. 2-1 to 2-6.

Guidelines for Writing Result and Duty Statements

- Describe the results and duties as they should be performed, not as you would like them to be performed or as the person currently in the position performs them.
- List results and duties rather than using a narrative paragraph format.
- Use the present tense.
- Arrange results and duties in a logical order beginning with the most important.
- Use active rather than passive verbs (Table 2-2).
- Avoid the use of verbs such as *ensure* or *provide*, and be specific when writing duty statements.
- Avoid discussing exactly how duties are supposed to be performed, as this information should be in an operations or policies and procedures manual. Instead, state "according to policies and procedures" or "using standard practice."
- Indicate how often each duty must be performed.
- Explain the extent of authority and responsibility involved.
- Explain the extent of supervision that will be received during performance of the duties.

Table 2-2 Specific Active Verbs for Job Descriptions

Compare

check	index	revise
proofread	classify	verify
edit	affirm	rate
catalogue		

Contact

call	interview	conduct
notify	refer	facilitate
visit	attend	consult
inform	collaborate	confer
correspond	participate	request
discuss	cooperate	requisition

Control

decide	schedule	employ
determine	select	secure
direct	assign	obtain
authorize	act for	contract
sign	act	require
approve	order	follow up
assume	initiate	expedite
conduct	implement	correct
execute	release	keep
delegate	oversee	ensure
represent	arrange	maintain
manage	anticipate	cancel
supervise	coordinate	close
administer	route	adopt

Count

add	inventory	remit
total	measure	disburse
balance	calculate	sell
bill	reconcile	collect
invoice	compute	appraise
figure	compile	evaluate
extend	pay	

Design

develop	institute	create
plan	elect	originate
organize	define	formulate
establish	prepare	

Operate

center	carry	feed
align	handle	type
clear	collate	process
stack	dissemble	batch
open	assemble	sort

Recommend

advise	submit	promote
apprise	suggest	contribute
consult	propose	interpret
counsel		

Record

register	disseminate	merge
receive	list	place
code	issue	file
note	furnish	transfer
describe	render	tabulate
outline	post	chart
summarize	prepare	lay out
write	process	amend
compose	enter	locate
draft	attach	find
copy	delete	trace
circulate	itemize	consolidate
distribute	arrange	

Study

examine	ascertain	test
audit	inspect	survey
investigate	observe	scan
analyze	sample	screen
review	estimate	search

Teach

train	instruct	guide

Source: From *Building a Fair Pay Program,* Copyright 1986 Roger J. Plachy. Published by AMACOM, a division of American Management Association, New York. Reprinted by permission. All rights reserved.

- Mention resources used in performing the job duties, such as cooking equipment, calculators, and so forth. You may want to list tools and equipment separately.

You may want to put the percentage of working time that should be devoted to each result and duty alongside it to indicate its importance.

Included in most job descriptions is a statement to the effect that the employee "performs other job duties as needed." This statement is put in to allow for emergencies and changing work conditions.

JOB SETTING

The section on job setting describes the conditions under which the job is to be done and normally covers

Personal contacts both within and outside the operation
Physical conditions, such as temperature, humidity, noise, and ventilation
Physical demands, such as heavy lifting
Personal demands, such as stress
Work hazards, such as back injuries

JOB QUALIFICATIONS

Up to this point, the job description has described the job. Now it is time to describe the person who will occupy this job.

In thinking of what is required to do a job, part of the process should include separating those qualifications that are needed to do the job minimally from those that may be considered desirable. For example, you may desire all your employees, including your dishwashers, to have a high school diploma. However, dishwashing, as well as some other jobs, can certainly be done very well by employees who do not have a high school diploma. Qualifications must be determined based on the actual duties and needs of the job, not the preferences of the employer. You may, however, state in this section of the job description that a qualification is "preferred but not required" and, instead, spell out the knowledge and skill level you are seeking. In this manner, you will not disqualify an applicant who can do the job but lacks a diploma.

This section of the job description should discuss qualifications in four areas:

1. Knowledge
2. Skills and abilities

3. Work experience
4. Education and training

Knowledge consists of the information needed to perform job duties. Knowledge statements may begin with verbs such as knows, defines, lists, describes, or explains. For example, a storekeeper needs to know different can sizes. A cook needs to be able to describe how to tell doneness in a whole baked chicken.

Skills and abilities consist of being able, or competent, to perform a task and to have appropriate work behavior. Tasks have already been listed in the job description. The following list covers other skills and abilities needed for various foodservice jobs.

- Is reliable and dependable
- Dresses according to policy
- Communicates well orally
- Listens
- Works well with coworkers
- Works well with guests
- Is flexible
- Writes legibly
- Works as part of a team
- Solves problems
- Is able to learn
- Works independently
- Handles stress
- Takes pride in work
- Works hard
- Has a positive attitude
- Is energetic
- Is honest

When writing skills and abilities, it is best to show the link between the qualification and the specific task to be performed, such as "Writes guest checks legibly and according to standard."

Generally a minimum level of work experience is required for many positions. Employers often equate experience with ability, as well as with attitude, figuring that someone who has done the job before and is applying for a similar job, must enjoy the work and do it well.

Employers may also specify minimum levels of formal education and types of education. Formal education can indicate ability or skills present.

3

Legal Aspects
of Staffing

The staffing process is the most important part of the human resources function and is more vulnerable to lawsuits than firing an employee. It is therefore very important to have an understanding of the legal aspects; however, because there are both federal and state laws on staffing which do change from time to time, it is recommended that you get advice from a skilled lawyer who is familiar with the requirements of your state.

Equal Employment Opportunity Laws

Table 3-1 lists important federal laws and executive orders regarding staffing and, in particular, employment discrimination. The intent of this group of laws and executive orders, referred to as Equal Employment Opportunity (EEO) laws, is the employment of certain classes of individuals in a fair and nondiscriminatory manner. Federal EEO laws prohibit discrimination on the basis of race, color, religion, sex, nationality, age, or handicap.

Besides federal laws, state and local governments also have fair employment practice acts (FEP). They are patterned after federal legislation and often extend antidiscrimination laws to businesses with just one or more employees. They might expand the definition of discrimination to include such factors as physical appearance or marital status. State and local agencies, such as the Michigan Depart-

Table 3-1 Federal Laws and Executive Orders Regarding Staffing

Federal Laws and Executive Orders	Type of Employment Discrimination Prohibited	Employers Covered
Equal Pay Act of 1963	Sex differences in pay, fringe benefits, and pension for substantially equal work	Private
Title VII, 1964 Civil Rights Act	Discrimination in all human resource activities based on race, color, sex, religion, or national origin; established Equal Employment Opportunity Commission to administer the law	Private; federal, state, and local governments; unions; employment agencies
Age Discrimination in Employment Act of 1967 (as amended in 1986)	Age discrimination against those 40 years of age or older	Private; unions; employment agencies
Executive Order 11478 (1969)	Discrimination based on race, color, religion, sex, national origin, political affiliation, marital status, or physical handicap	Federal government
Equal Employment Opportunity Act of 1972	Amended Title VII; gave Equal Employment Opportunity Commission (EEOC) more power to enforce and extended coverage	Educational institutions; other employers
Vocational Rehabilitation Act of 1973, Executive Order 11914 (1974)	Discrimination based on physical or mental handicap	Federal government and federal contractors
Vietnam Era Veterans Readjustment Act of 1974	Discrimination against disabled veterans and Vietnam veterans	Same as above

Table 3-1   Continued

Federal Laws and Executive Orders	Type of Employment Discrimination Prohibited	Employers Covered
Pregnancy Discrimination Act of 1978	Discrimination in hiring, promoting, or terminating because of pregnancy; pregnancy to be treated as a medical disability	Same as Title VII
Immigration Reform and Control Act (1986)	Requires employer to verify identity and eligibility of new hires using Form I-9	Must be done on all new hires
Americans with Disabilities Act of 1990	Discrimination of disabled individuals in hiring and employment	Businesses with over 25 employees, by 1992, businesses with 15 or more employees
Fair Employment Practice Acts of States and Local Governments	Discrimination of various types	Varies

ment of Civil Rights, are set up to administer the fair employment practice acts. The appendix lists each state's labor department.

The earliest EEO law dates back to Section 1981 of the Civil Rights Act of 1866, which guarantees all persons, regardless of race, the right to make and enforce contracts, such as the employment contract. There have been numerous laws passed since then, such as Title VII of the Civil Rights Act of 1964, which is the principal piece of federal legislation addressing employment discrimination. It makes it unlawful for an employer to discriminate against applicants or employees with respect to hiring, firing, promotions, or compensation on the basis of race, color, religion, sex, national origin, or age. Title VII does not, however, require employers to hire, promote, or keep employees who are not qualified.

Title VII created the Equal Employment Opportunity Commission (EEOC) to administer and to enforce the law. The EEOC has jurisdiction over businesses with 15 or more workers. In 1978 the EEOC and three other government agencies — the Civil Service Commission, the Department of Labor, and the Department of Justice — presented a unified federal position on nondiscriminatory employment practices: the Uniform Guidelines of Employee Selection Procedures. This document applies to private employers who employ 15 or more employees for 20 or more weeks in a calendar year, as well as to federal, state, and local governments. It was designed primarily to show employers how to comply with EEO laws. It also asks employers to demonstrate that selection procedures are job-related and valid; that is, they are able to predict good job performance.

Title VII allows an employer to hire individuals of a particular religion, sex, or nationality only if the decision is based on a bona fide occupational qualification (BFOQ). For example, an attendant in a men's restroom has to be male. In order to meet legal requirements, a BFOQ must be a business necessity; in other words, the business would be negatively affected without such an exemption from the law. In general, the EEOC and the courts do not approve a BFOQ unless there is a very strong case for its use, such as safety. Race and color can never be a bona fide occupational qualification.

Other important antidiscrimination legislation includes the

Age Discrimination in Employment Act of 1967 (amended in 1986)
Equal Pay Act of 1963
Pregnancy Discrimination Act of 1978
Americans with Disabilities Act of 1990

As amended in 1986, the Age Discrimination in Employment Act of 1967 makes it unlawful for an employer to discriminate against applicants or employees who are over 40 years of age because of the person's age. It does not prohibit discrimination against individuals under 40 years of age, although some states do protect other age groups.

The Equal Pay Act of 1963 requires equal pay, fringe benefits, and pensions for men and women who work in jobs that require substantially equal skills, effort, and responsibilities under similar working conditions. This law protects women only and applies to all aspects of employment, such as starting salaries and annual salary increases. In order for an employee to claim violation of the Equal Pay Act, identical job classifications must be compared.

According to the Pregnancy Discrimination Act of 1978, employers cannot discriminate against a woman on the basis of pregnancy or childbirth. In the case of selection, an employer cannot refuse to hire a woman just because she is pregnant. Pregnancy is to be seen as a temporary disability, and women must be permitted to work as long as they are able to do their jobs.

The Americans with Disabilities Act of 1990 bars bias in employment against the estimated 43 million Americans who have a physical or a mental disability. It defines a disability as a condition that "substantially limits" a "major life activity," like walking or seeing. It covers recovering drug abusers and alcoholics but not a host of other emotional disorders, like kleptomania or compulsive gambling. It also covers, for the first time, people who have acquired immune deficiency syndrome (AIDS) or who are infected with the AIDS virus.

During the first 2 years after its enactment in 1990, businesses with more than 25 employees are forbidden to discriminate against qualified individuals who have a disability when they are hired. Businesses will also be required to change their physical plants to make a "reasonable accommodation" to disabled employees so they can do their jobs. Examples of "reasonable accommodation" in a foodservice are outfitting point-of-sale systems with braille keys, lowering a work table so someone can work while seated, or changing job schedules, job duties, policies, and training procedures. Employers will be exempt from this condition if they can prove undue hardship on the business, which means a remedy requiring significant expense. In the third year of the bill, it will be enforced in work places with 15 or more employees.

EEO LAWS AND THE STAFFING PROCESS

According to the EEOC, job qualifications and selection procedures must be job-related and valid, meaning they are able to predict good job performance. Selection procedures, such as applications and interviews, must be in compliance with the Uniform Guidelines on Employee Selection Procedures and must not result in adverse impact on any race, sex, or ethnic group.

"Adverse impact" refers to a substantially different rate of selection in hiring (or other employment decisions, such as promotions) that works to the disadvantage of members of a particular group. Adverse impact is determined to have taken place, in some cases, if the selection rate for any group is less than 80 percent of the rate for the group with the highest rate of selection, which is usually white males. For example, if 10 out of 50 white applicants (or 20 percent) are selected for a job, at least 16 percent of minority candidates (80 percent of 20) should be selected so the employer will not be accused of adverse impact. Adverse impact is considered only for groups that constitute more than 2 percent of the relevant labor force.

You need to be able to answer "yes" to the following questions about your selection procedures.

1. Will this requested information help to judge the applicant's ability to do the job? Is every part of the selection procedures job-related?
2. Will each part of the selection process, including job descriptions, applications, and interviews, prevent screening out those groups covered by EEO laws?
3. Is the selection process consistently applied to all applicants?

In addition to the requirements of the EEOC, there are certain preemployment inquiries and processes that are limited by many states.

Table 3-2 reviews recommended ways to ask questions of job applicants, whether concerning job applications or during interviews, or any other technique, to avoid charges of discrimination. Asking questions such as "Do you have children?" are often legal; however, once such information has been received, employers may be charged with using it to discriminate against women. When answers to questions such as the number of children or race are needed for tax, insurance, Social Security, or EEO reporting purposes, it is recommended that this information be obtained after the employee has been hired.

In addition to the information given in Table 3-2, the following information is important.

- An employer is obligated to make a reasonable accommodation to employees' religious beliefs, unless it causes an undue economic hardship on the business. For example, if an employee needs Sundays off and it is possible to change the employee's schedule without undue hardship, the employer should accommodate the employee. Just what constitutes an undue hardship depends on various factors, such as prohibitive cost. Generally, the larger the company, the more the employer is expected to spend to accommodate an employee. If a case is taken to court, undue hardship must be proven.
- The ability to speak English is a valid job requirement when it is necessary to converse with customers or other employees. However, if English is not essential in order for the job to be performed, the employee cannot be required to speak it.
- Concerning asking applicants about prior arrests and convictions, the EEOC permits an employer to consider such information

when there is a direct relationship between an applicant's arrest or conviction and his or her fitness for a particular job. However, some states prohibit employers from asking about prior arrests, and some states prohibit discrimination against applicants with arrest or conviction records. The reason for this is that some minority groups are arrested and convicted more frequently than whites, so if a selection decision is based on arrest or conviction records, employment opportunities will be disproportionately limited for these groups.

- Unless business necessity can be proved, it is not appropriate for an employer to use an applicant's financial status when making an employment decision. Practices such as asking whether the applicant owns or rents a residence, how long an applicant has lived at an address, or whether the applicant owns a car should be avoided. There is no evidence that applicants with credit problems will be poor employees or will be more likely to steal. In addition, it is probable that this practice would discriminate against some minority groups.

Any type of preemployment tests that are used must meet guidelines for nondiscrimination according to Title VII and the EEO Uniform Guidelines on Employee Selection Procedures:

An employer can act upon the results of any professionally developed test provided that such test . . . is not designed, intended or used to discriminate because of race, color, religion, sex or national origin. (Title VII of the Civil Rights Act)

Test refers to any screening device used in employee selection. Any test used, whether it measures strength, personality, knowledge, ability, or aptitude, must bear a reasonable relationship to successful performance on the job; that is, it should be validated. It should also be administered to all applicants. More on the legality of testing is covered in Chapter 7, "Evaluating Applicants."

Job requirements or qualifications, such as those regarding education and experience, must be job-related, nondiscriminatory, and predictive of future job performance. Although requiring a high school diploma for an entry-level foodservice job, such as a server, seems to be acceptable, there are certainly many servers who can do the job satisfactorily who lack a diploma. In addition, the requirement of a high school diploma has a greater negative impact on minority members, so it may be viewed as discriminatory. It is better to state that a diploma is desirable and to specify the specific knowledge and skills needed to do the job.

Table 3-2   Questions for Job Applicants

Subject	Inappropriate	Suggested
Name	What is your maiden name? Have you ever used any other last name?	What is your full name? Have you ever worked or attended school under a different name?
Address	Do you rent or own?	What is your address?
Age	What is your date of birth? What is your age? What are the dates you attended school?	Are you 18 years of age or older? What schools have you attended?
Sex	Are you male or female?	No inquiries unless BFOQ.
Marital Status	Are you married, divorced, separated, or single? What is your spouse's name?	No inquiries.
Children	Are you pregnant, or do you intend to become pregnant? Do you have any children?	No inquiries.
Race and National Origin	What is your race? Where were you born? What is your native language?	No inquiries. (If job-related) What foreign languages do you speak fluently?
Citizen	Of what country are you a citizen? Are you a native-born U.S. citizen? When did you acquire your citizenship?	Are you a U.S. citizen? Do you have the legal right to live and work in the United States? For how long?

Table 3-2 Continued

Subject	Inappropriate	Suggested
Appearance	What is the color of your hair, eyes, and skin? Please send me a photograph.	No inquiries unless BFOQ.
Religion	What is your religious affiliation? Which religious holidays do you observe?	Can you work on the days required by this job?
Health	What is your health status? Do you have any physical or mental disabilities? Have you had any recent or past illnesses or operations? What is the date of your last physical exam?	Do you have any health concerns that might interfere with your ability to do this job? Are you willing to take a physical if the nature of the job requires one?
Notify in Emergency	Whom should we notify in case of an emergency? What is your relationship to this person?	Whom should we notify in case of an emergency?
Member of Groups	Are you a member of any groups or organizations?	Do you belong to any job-related groups or organizations?
Education	Are you a high school graduate?	What is the highest grade that you completed?

AFFIRMATIVE-ACTION PROGRAMS

Affirmative-action programs go beyond EEO. Affirmative action is a policy that requires organizations to correct past discriminatory practices by making extra efforts to recruit, hire, and promote qualified women, minorities, and other groups protected by EEO laws. This is implemented by having organizations set up affirmative-action programs as follows in order to ensure a balanced and representative work force (Equal Employment Opportunity Commission, 1974):

1. Issue written equal employment policy and affirmative-action commitment
2. Appoint a top official with responsibility and authority to direct and implement the program
3. Publicize the policy and affirmative-action commitment
4. Survey present minority and female employment by department and job classification
5. Develop goals and timetables to improve utilization of minorities, males, and females in each area where utilization has been identified
6. Develop and implement specific programs to achieve goals
7. Establish an internal audit and reporting system to monitor and evaluate progress in each aspect of the program
8. Develop supportive in-house and community programs

Affirmative-action programs are required for employers with federal contracts over a certain amount, as well as employers who have been found guilty of discriminatory employment practices. Such programs are also freely developed by some employers.

WHEN AN EMPLOYEE CHARGES DISCRIMINATION

An employee can file a charge of discrimination, referred to as an "unfair employment practice," with a state or local Equal Employment Opportunity agency, as well as with the EEOC. If there is no state or local agency, the employee must file with the EEOC. After the charge has been filed, the employer is notified and a fact-finding conference is set up. At this conference, both parties are allowed to state their cases, and an EEOC agent tries to settle the issues, if possible. Many cases are resolved at this point.

If the case is not resolved, an investigation takes place, the results of which are communicated to both parties. At this point, the employee is also given a "right-to-sue" letter, which gives the employee the right to take the case to court. If the employee does file a lawsuit, he or she carries the burden of proving that discrimination did, indeed, take place.

The address for the EEOC's national offices is

Equal Employment Opportunity Commission
2401 E Street, N.W.
Washington, DC 20506

Appendix A lists the Human Relations Commissions in most states.

The Fair Labor Standards Act

The Fair Labor Standards Act (FLSA), commonly referred to as the Wage and Hour Law, establishes minimum wage, overtime pay, record keeping, and child labor standards, as well as other regulations. It applies to all foodservices with gross annual retail sales of $500,000 or more, exclusive of excise taxes. The FLSA is enforced by the U.S. Department of Labor, Employment Standards Administration, Wage and Hour Division.

Effective April 1, 1991, the minimum wage is $4.25. Employees of foodservices with gross annual retail sales of between $362,500 and $500,000 must receive $3.35 or more per hour. If the state has a higher minimum wage, the higher rate must be paid.

A training wage of at least $3.61 can be paid, effective April 1, 1991, under certain conditions.

- The employee must be under the age of 20.
- The period during which the training wage is paid is not to exceed 90 days.
- The employer must give the employee a written notice explaining the training wage and its requirements before the employee starts work.
- The employer cannot displace an employee from his or her job and then hire someone who will be paid a training wage.

Effective March 31, 1993, employees cannot be paid a training wage.

The Fair Labor Standards Act also addresses the issue of child labor. For minors (under 18 years of age), there are laws restricting maximum work hours, night work, and jobs involving certain types of equipment and the serving of alcoholic beverages. The federal child labor laws are described below; however, if a state or local law is stricter than the federal one, the state or local law must be followed.

Minimum Employment Age: 14 years of age
Minors 14 and 15 years of age may not do any of the following:
  Cooking (except at soda fountains, lunch counters, snack bars, or cafeteria serving counters) or baking
  Work requiring the use of a ladder
  Occupations that involve operating, setting up, adjusting, cleaning, oiling, or repairing power-driven food slicers and grinders, food choppers and cutters, or bakery-type mixers
  Work in freezers or meat coolers or in preparation of meats for sale (except wrapping, sealing, labeling, weighing, pricing, or stocking when performed in other areas)
  Loading and unloading goods to and from trucks, railroad cars, or conveyors
  Work in warehouses, except office or clerical work
Minors 16 and 17 years of age may not do any of the following (with certain exceptions for students):
  Operate elevators or power-driven hoists
  Operate power-driven shearing machines or bakery machinery
  Operate circular saws or band saws
  Drive certain motor vehicles (without restrictions)

Maximum Work Hours:
  Ages 14 and 15: on school days, 3 hours per day, 18 hours per week; on nonschool days, 8 hours per day, 40 hours per week. Also, work may not begin before 7 A.M. or end after 7 P.M., except from June 1 through Labor Day, when evening hours are extended to 9 P.M.
  Ages 16 and over: no restrictions on work hours

An operator may be fined up to $10,000 for a willful first violation of the child labor standards. If the operator has been convicted twice for similar offenses, the penalty is up to $10,000 or up to 6 months in jail, or both. In 1990, the Department of Labor started to crack down on foodservice operators who were employing minors illegally.

The FLSA also explains the concept of "exempt" and "nonexempt" employees. Employees working in executive, administrative, or professional positions are considered "exempt" employees, meaning that they are exempt from minimum wage and overtime parts of the law. To be exempt, the employee must

Manage a company or a department within the company

Supervise two or more employees

Be able to hire and fire employees, or to make recommendations to do so that are seriously considered

Receive a salary of at least $155 per week

Be responsible primarily for management duties, with no more than 40 percent of the employee's work time spent performing nonexempt work

Be able to regularly use discretion in his or her work

The Department of Labor also recognizes as exempt the manager of a foodservice who is solely in charge but spends more than 40 percent of his or her time doing nonexempt work. However, only one manager per establishment can be considered as exempt.

Immigration Reform and Control Act (1986)

Under the Immigration Reform and Control Act (IRCA), it is illegal for an employer to knowingly hire or continue to employ an illegal alien or to hire anyone without verifying his or her identity and employment eligibility. An illegal alien is someone who either did not legally enter the United States or does not have authorization to work in the United States. Under this law, an employer also cannot discriminate against aliens because of their citizenship. The Civil Rights Act of 1964 prohibits employers who have at least 15 employees from discriminating against employees based on national origin. The IRCA prohibits employers who have more than 3 but fewer than 15 employees from discriminating against employees based on citizenship.

Aliens are not permitted to work while they are in the United States unless they come under a special category in the federal Immigration and Nationality Act. For example, lawful permanent resident aliens and political refugees are allowed to work. Also, aliens may be allowed to work temporarily or permanently in certain jobs if qualified Americans are not available to do the work. An alien can make an application for permanent employment at an office of the Immigration and Naturalization Service for jobs for which there are not enough qualified Americans. An employer can also apply for this certification through the local Job Service Office. A Job Service Office is a public employment agency and is discussed in more detail in Chapter 6. If the employer applies for an alien to take a job for which there are enough Americans, the employer must show documentation of his or her efforts to recruit Americans. The Job Service Office will then try to recruit people for the job before approving the permanent certification.

Under the Immigration Reform and Control Act, employers must verify the identity and employment eligibility of all individuals hired after November 6, 1986 who continued to be employed after May 31, 1987. This is accomplished by filling out Form I-9, Employment Eligibility Verification (Fig. 3-1) which takes about 20 minutes to complete. Section 1 of the form should be filled out by the employee, and Section 2 should be filled out by the employer. In Section 2, the employee needs to give the employer either one document from List A to establish identity and employment eligibility or one document from List B (to establish identity) and List C (to establish employment eligibility).

Documents from List A include

U.S. passport
Certificate of U.S. Citizenship (INS Form N-560 or N-561)
Certificate of Naturalization (INS Form N-550 or N-570)
Unexpired foreign passport with attached Employment Authorization Card
Alien Registration Receipt Card (INS Form I-151) or Resident Alien Card (INS Form I-551) with photograph
Temporary Resident Card (INS Form I-688)
Employment Authorization Card (INS Form I-688A)

Under List B, documents which establish identity include

A state-issued driver's license or a state-issued I.D. card with a photograph, or information, including name, sex, date of birth, height, weight, and color of eyes
U.S. military card or draft record
School identification card with photograph
Voter's registration card
Identification card issued by a federal, state, or local government agency
Military dependent's identification card
Canadian driver's license

If an employee is under 18 years of age, the employee may accept a school record, such as a report card; a physician, clinic, or hospital record; or a day-care or nursery school record.

Fig. 3-1 FORM I-9

EMPLOYMENT ELIGIBILITY VERIFICATION (Form I-9)

1 EMPLOYEE INFORMATION AND VERIFICATION: (To be completed and signed by employee.)

Name: (Print or Type) Last	First	Middle	Birth Name

Address: Street Name and Number	City	State	ZIP Code

Date of Birth (Month/Day/Year)	Social Security Number

I attest, under penalty of perjury, that I am (check a box):

☐ 1. A citizen or national of the United States.
☐ 2. An alien lawfully admitted for permanent residence (Alien Number A _____)
☐ 3. An alien authorized by the Immigration and Naturalization Service to work in the United States (Alien Number A _____ ,
or Admission Number _____ , expiration of employment authorization, if any _____) .

I attest, under penalty of perjury, the documents that I have presented as evidence of identity and employment eligibility are genuine and relate to me. I am aware that federal law provides for imprisonment and/or fine for any false statements or use of false documents in connection with this certificate.

Signature	Date (Month/Day/Year)

PREPARER/TRANSLATOR CERTIFICATION (To be completed if prepared by person other than the employee). I attest, under penalty of perjury, that the above was prepared by me at the request of the named individual and is based on all information of which I have any knowledge.

Signature	Name (Print or Type)		
Address (Street Name and Number)	City	State	Zip Code

2 EMPLOYER REVIEW AND VERIFICATION: (To be completed and signed by employer.)

Instructions:
Examine one document from List A and check the appropriate box, **OR** examine one document from List B **and** one from List C and check the appropriate boxes. Provide the **Document Identification Number** and **Expiration Date** for the document checked.

List A Documents that Establish Identity and Employment Eligibility	List B Documents that Establish Identity	and	List C Documents that Establish Employment Eligibility
☐ 1. United States Passport	☐ 1. A State-issued driver's license or a State-issued I.D. card with a photograph, or information, including name, sex, date of birth, height, weight, and color of eyes. (Specify State)_____		☐ 1. Original Social Security Number Card (other than a card stating it is not valid for employment)
☐ 2. Certificate of United States Citizenship			
☐ 3. Certificate of Naturalization	☐ 2. U.S. Military Card		☐ 2. A birth certificate issued by State, county, or municipal authority bearing a seal or other certification
☐ 4. Unexpired foreign passport with attached Employment Authorization	☐ 3. Other (Specify document and issuing authority)		☐ 3. Unexpired INS Employment Authorization Specify form
☐ 5. Alien Registration Card with photograph			# _____
Document Identification	**Document Identification**		**Document Identification**
# _____	# _____		# _____
Expiration Date (if any)	**Expiration Date (if any)**		**Expiration Date (if any)**

CERTIFICATION: I attest, under penalty of perjury, that I have examined the documents presented by the above individual, that they appear to be genuine and to relate to the individual named, and that the individual, to the best of my knowledge, is eligible to work in the United States.

Signature	Name (Print or Type)	Title
Employer Name	Address	Date

Form I-9 (05/07/87)
OMB No. 1115-0136

U.S. Department of Justice
Immigration and Naturalization Service

Under List C, documents that establish employment eligibility include

Original Social Security Card, other than a card stating it is "not valid for employment purposes"
An original or certified birth certificate issued by a state, county, or municipal authority bearing a seal or other certification
Unexpired Immigration and Naturalization Service Employment Authorization
Reentry permit (INS Form I-327) (check expiration date)
Refugee Travel Document (INS Form I-571) (check expiration date)
Certification of Birth Abroad (Form DS-1350) or Certification of Birth (Form FS-545), both issued by the Department of State
United States Citizen Identification Card (INS Form I-197)
Identification Card for use of Resident Citizen in the United States (INS Form I-179)

Form I-9 must be filled out completely by the employer and by the new employee within three business days of the hire date and kept on file for 3 years or for 1 year after an employee has been terminated, whichever is later. The new employee must supply documents to establish identity and employment eligibility, as listed on Form I-9. Although employers are not required to keep copies of the documentation presented, if documentation is kept for one employee, it should be kept for all employees.

If the paperwork is not done correctly, there is a penalty of between $100 to $1,000 for each individual. In cases in which unauthorized aliens have been knowingly hired or continue to be employed, the first offense is penalized by a $250 to $2,000 fine, the second offense by a $2,000 to $5,000 fine, and any further offenses by a $3,000 to $10,000 fine. Imprisonment is possible if a pattern of offenses develops.

When an employer has more than one unit which is physically separate from the other(s), each unit is considered to be a separate employer if each handles its own hiring without any company guidance or control.

More information about the employment of aliens can be obtained from

Division of Labor Certification
U.S. Employment Service
601 D Street, N.W.
Washington, DC 20213

The Immigration and Naturalization Service provides information on completing the I-9 form in their *INS Handbook for Employers.*

Employee Polygraph Protection Act

The Employee Polygraph Protection Act of 1988 forbids the use of a lie detector to screen job applicants or at any point in the employment process. A polygraph is an instrument that simultaneously records changes in physiological process, such as heartbeat, blood pressure, and respiration, and is sometimes used in lie detection. Polygraphs, as well as any other similar devices which diagnostically determine the honesty of an individual, cannot be requested or required of a prospective or current employee.

There is one exemption to this law and that is when an employer is investigating theft or injury to the business. In these cases, the employer must have reasonable suspicion of the employee and must meet other requirements before doing such a test.

Negligent Hiring

If the selection process is neglected and employers make a practice of hiring just "warm bodies," they are leaving themselves open to being sued for negligent hiring, in addition to undesirable results, such as high turnover rates and poor-quality products and services. In the past 10 years, lawsuits for negligent hiring have increased tremendously. Guests or other employees who become injured by a violent or hostile employee may sue the employer for negligently hiring or retaining such an employee. If the injured party can prove that the hostile employee should not have been hired or retained, the employer is found liable. Unfortunately, in the foodservice industry, the risk of negligent hiring and retention is much greater due to large numbers of employees, much customer contact, and a high turnover rate.

The employer has the duty of due care, which means taking reasonable and appropriate precautions to avoid hiring and retaining employees who might harm other workers or the public, as, for instance, in assault and battery. To avoid liability for negligent hiring, the employer can

Have each applicant fill out an employment application
Conduct a thorough background check of job applicants; verify
    employment and education; ask the applicant to sign a waiver

and release form for consent to do complete reference checks from former employers (see Chapter 7).

Look for gaps in employment and short residency periods and ask the applicant for explanations for such gaps

Examine state laws on hiring applicants with criminal records; ask on the application if the applicant has ever been convicted of a criminal offense; check for a criminal record if warranted by the nature of the position

Ask, when checking out work references, about problem behavior, such as violence, inability to get along with others, lying, and excessive absenteeism or lateness.

Keep written documentation of all telephone reference checks

Record Keeping and Posting Requirements

In addition to the federal requirements noted in this section, there are state laws which may require keeping additional records or posting additional requirements, or both.

EQUAL EMPLOYMENT OPPORTUNITY

Employers who employ over 100 employees must submit annually a report referred to as the Employer Information Report EEO-1. In this report, all employees are first classified into job categories, and each job category is separated into a gender and minority status. In order to obtain the data needed for this report, employers are allowed to collect minority group data on job applicants as long as any form requesting such information is kept separate from the application. The EEO-1 report is examined by the EEOC in the event of a discrimination claim.

To be prepared for possible claims of discrimination and to show support for equal employment opportunity, employers should keep records of all recruitment efforts for 1 year, including advertisements, referral sources, and so on. Title VII requires retention of all employment and personnel records, including applications, for 6 months, unless the applicant is over 40 years of age, in which case records must be kept for 1 year. It is advisable simply to save all records for at least 1 year.

If a company is subject to the EEOC regulations, the employer must conspicuously post in the company a notice about prohibited discrimination. To obtain a poster, contact a regional office of the EEOC or call 800-USA-EEOC.

TWO

Recruiting

EMPLOYEE FILES

Once an employee has been hired, an employee file must be started. According to the FLSA, the following information must be maintained for each employee:

Full name
Home address with zip code
Social Security number
Date of birth, if under 19 years of age
Sex
Job title or occupation
Day of week when workweek begins
Wages or salary

Special certificates, such as those for employees who are eligible for the Targeted Jobs Tax Credit, discussed in Chapter 6, should be kept on file. Certificates should be retained for 3 years from the most recent effective date.

FAIR LABOR STANDARDS ACT

If the FLSA applies to a business, the employer needs to post a notice conspicuously that explains minimum wage and other aspects of the FLSA. To obtain a poster, contact a regional office of the Department of Labor or call 202-523-7043.

EMPLOYEE POLYGRAPH PROTECTION ACT

According to Department of Labor regulations, an employer also needs to post a notice conspicuously that explains the Employee Polygraph Protection Act of 1988. To obtain a poster, contact a regional office of the Department of Labor.

4

Introduction to Recruiting

Recruiting is a set of activities used by companies to attract qualified job applicants. In this chapter we will start with a discussion of internal and external recruiting, and then we will consider prerequisites to recruiting, including types of incentives foodservice employers are offering applicants.

Internal and External Recruiting

Recruiting is typically categorized as being "internal" or "external." "Internal recruiting" refers to informing current employees about job openings so that they may apply for them. For example, an employee may find out, perhaps informally in conversation or formally through departmental mail, that a position is open within an organization. If the employee is interested in the position, especially if it represents a promotion, the employee may want to apply. Likewise, a current employee may want to take a new position in a different area for a new challenge or as a change of pace.

Whereas internal recruiting refers to seeking job applicants from within, "external recruiting" refers to the process of seeking job applicants from outside the operation. Foodservice managers have become very creative in their outside recruiting efforts, and some of their novel techniques will be discussed in Chapter 6.

Internal recruiting has several advantages. It rewards and motivates current employees, giving them something to work toward. In this manner, it can help decrease employee turnover. It also provides for continuity and consistency within the operation. While it is faster and less expensive than other methods, it does create another vacant job which must then be filled.

External recruiting likewise has advantages. People coming into the company from the outside bring in new ideas and a fresh perspective. They are less likely to accept the attitude that "it's always been done this way," and they are more likely to help other staff members see situations in a different light. It is a good idea for an employer to fill at least some management positions with outside applicants.

Prerequisites to Recruiting

Recruiting high-caliber employees involves four prerequisites.

1. You need to contribute to your community and be visible in your community.
2. You need to create a good impression when applicants come into your company.
3. You need to provide incentives such as competitive wages and benefits.
4. You need to have a good reputation. As an employer, you should be known for being a good employer and for providing a pleasant work environment. A reputation for being a poor place to work will seriously affect your ability to recruit good people.

Of course, having a good reputation will only help bring applicants to your door. What are employees looking for? In *The 100 Best Companies to work for in America*, companies rated highest by their employees tend to

Make employees feel that they belong to a team or a family
Encourage open communication
Stress quality and make employees feel proud about the product or
    service they produce
Minimize distinctions of rank between management and entry-level
    employees
Create as agreeable and pleasant a working environment as possible
Promote from within
Increase the skill level of employees through training programs and
    tuition reimbursement
Permit employees to share in the profits of the company

CONTRIBUTE TO THE COMMUNITY AND BE VISIBLE

In addition to taking care of your employees, it is also important to contribute to the community in which you are operating. Whenever you do something for the community, you are also getting visibility. Probably the most well-known examples are McDonald's Ronald McDonald Houses. These are homes which provide temporary housing for families of very sick children, such as those with cancer, who are receiving medical treatment at a nearby hospital.

Following are examples of how you might be able to give back to your community.

- Contribute food to a soup kitchen that prepares food for the homeless.
- Be involved in Toys for Tots.
- Ask your employees to be involved in a United Way campaign.
- Sponsor athletic teams.
- Sponsor public service anouncements.

It is also crucial to publicize what you have done. This can be accomplished through press releases or a customer newsletter.

GIVE A GOOD FIRST IMPRESSION

When applicants come in to inquire about jobs or for an interview, it is important for them to get a good first impression of your operation. This first impression will include how clean and orderly everything looks, how the applicants were greeted, and so on. Employees should know what to do when applicants come in and request an application.

Incentives to Attract Employees

Foodservice employers are offering various incentives to attract and retain employees. The following are some examples of incentives:

Competitive wages and benefits
Profit-sharing program
Pay-for-performance and pay-for-knowledge
Regular job evaluation and advancement
Training and orientation programs and manuals
Employee rewards

Relocation assistance
Transportation assistance
Child-care assistance
Sign-on bonus
Flexible hours
Alternative schedules
Parental leave
Tuition reimbursement
Free uniforms or uniform allowance
Free meals or meal allowance

In a survey done by the Gallup Organization for the National Restaurant Association in December 1989, foodservice managers reported offering the following incentives to retain hourly employees:

Flexible working schedules (90 percent)
On-going training (74 percent)
Advancement opportunities (65 percent)
Regular performance evaluations (60 percent)
Formal job training (60 percent)
Orientation program (59 percent)
Written job descriptions (47 percent)
Handbook explaining company policies (43 percent)
Benefits package (35 percent)

Any of these methods can also be used to recruit new employees.

It is important to check out what the competition is doing before you develop and offer your own set of incentives. It is also a good idea to determine how much money and time you have to devote to this type of program and to investigate the cost of various incentives. In order to find out the types of incentives which will attract potential employees to your operation, it is a good idea to query your current employees for ideas. For example, if the majority of your employees are college age, they may tell you that tuition assistance or flexible hours are very attractive. Also, examine your current incentives to see if any of them could be marketed to the applicant pool. Any incentives that you offer should be marketed right along with your jobs.

COMPETITIVE WAGES AND BENEFITS

In order to have competitive wages and benefits, you need to find out what your competition is offering. In response to the labor shortage and greater demand for employees, wages have been increasing.

Benefits were originally referred to as "fringe benefits" because they were quite meager and were given in addition to the paycheck. Their scope and costs have expanded widely. According to U.S. Chamber of Commerce surveys, costs of benefits have risen from 3 percent of total payroll expenses in 1929 to 36.6 percent in 1984. Of that 36.6 percent, approximately 10 percent is for legally required benefits, 11 percent for time not worked, and 8 percent to cover health and life insurance; the remaining 7.6 percent pays for other benefits and services. Categories of employee benefits which may be available are

LEGALLY REQUIRED BENEFITS
Social Security
Workers' Compensation
Unemployment Insurance

HEALTH AND LIFE INSURANCE
Group health insurance
Health Maintenance Organizations
Preferred Provider Organizations
Dental
Vision care
Prescription care
Group term life insurance
Accidental death and disability insurance
Long-term disability insurance
Short-term disability insurance

PENSIONS
Defined benefit
Defined contribution
   401(k) plan
   Profit-sharing
   Independent Retirement Account
Independent Retirement Account

PAYMENT FOR TIME NOT WORKED
Sick leave
Vacation time
Holidays
Bereavement
Breaks
Jury duty

EMPLOYEE SERVICES AND OTHER BENEFITS
Educational assistance
Credit unions
Meals
Uniforms
Employee assistance program
Wellness program
Social-recreational programs
Legal services
Discount purchases
Financial planning services
Preretirement planning and counseling
Relocation (moving) expenses
Child care
Membership in professional and trade associations
Scholarships for dependent children
Matched donations — universities and colleges

They include benefits that are legally required, health and life insurance, pensions, payment for time not worked, employee services, and other benefits.

Health insurance is the most common benefit offered in the United States. By far, a majority of employers offer health insurance to their employees. The National Restaurant Association's Survey of Health Insurance Coverage in the Restaurant Industry (1987) found that small companies are less likely to provide health insurance coverage. As sales volume increases, so does the possibility of providing coverage for salaried and hourly personnel. The most common features of health plans, when they are provided, include 90-day waiting periods, maximum coverage of $1 million, coverage of dependents, 30 to 40 hours per week of work required to qualify, and payment of 80 percent of the charges after the employee has paid the deductible.

The survey also found that the employer is now paying 50 percent more toward health insurance than in 1985. Likewise, there are more employers asking employees to contribute to payment of premiums.

Pensions are another area in which employers are devising plans in order to attract and retain employees. Most pension plans are categorized as defined benefit or defined contribution. In defined benefit plans, the amount of the pension upon retirement and the conditions for its payment are known ahead of time. In defined contribution plans, what is preset is how the employer and possibly the employee will contribute to the pension fund, which may be through profit sharing, Independent Retirement Accounts (IRA), or other ways. An

IRA is a tax shelter available under certain circumstances to individuals who normally use it as a source of retirement income. However, the amount of the actual pension is not determined until retirement, when the value of the funds invested is determined.

Among defined contribution plans, salary reduction or 401(k) plans, named after section 401(k) of the Internal Revenue Code, are the most popular. Employees, particularly in small businesses, can save for retirement through payroll deductions of from 1 to 6 percent of their paychecks, with the employer possibly matching their savings. All money contributed into the plan is tax deferred.

PROFIT SHARING

Profit sharing is the most popular type of gain-sharing plan. Gain-sharing plans are programs designed to provide an incentive for recruitment and retention, as well as high levels of productivity, through sharing the financial gains of the organization with employees. This involves any method that distributes a portion of the company's profits among the employees. Gain-sharing programs have been reported to have a positive effect on productivity and quality.

Profit sharing is often available to employees who have become eligible by reaching 21 years of age and who have worked 1,000 hours. In a cash plan, the profits are distributed annually. In a deferred plan, which is more common, there is no significant payment until termination, retirement, disability, or death. Some plans combine both cash and deferred concepts. According to a 1985 study for the National Restaurant Association (Boyle, 1987), 17 percent of restaurants had a form of profit sharing—a figure that was lower than that found in manufacturing (25 percent) and retail and wholesale (33 percent).

PAY-FOR-PERFORMANCE AND PAY-FOR-KNOWLEDGE

Pay-for-performance refers to a system of paying employees according to how well they perform their jobs. Merit raises are the most popular pay-for-performance method. Employees who believe that their efforts will be rewarded become productive and stay productive. Studies of both executives and employees show that when pay is tied to performance, employees' satisfaction, motivation, and productivity increase. For some people, increased pay uplifts their self-esteem, pride, and prestige.

The use of merit raises will fail to serve its motivational purpose if

Table 4-1 Sample Merit Increase Guidelines (by Percentage)

	Position in the Wage Range			
Performance Rating	Below 25	Below 50	Below 75	Below 90
Outstanding	15	12	9	6
Good	13	10	7	4
Meets standards	10	7	4	2
Below standards	No raise until performance is brought up to "Meets			
Unsatisfactory	standards."			

If the current wage is between 90 and 99 percent of the wage range, the increase will be to the maximum of the range. For employees who are already at the top of the wage range, a lump sum will be paid.

The performance evaluation system is not functioning effectively
Employees do not trust the managers who make the decisions that will affect their merit raises
Managers make their decisions based on favoritism, seniority, or pity
Employees can successfully pressure their supervisor to give them a higher-increase

Table 4-1 provides an example of merit guidelines. Depending on the rating given the employee and his or her position in the wage range within a particular class, wages will increase by a certain percentage. In some cases, the raise is given in a single amount, called a "lump-sum payment"; this is often used for employees who are red-circled, which means that their wage rate is at the maximum for their grade.

Related to pay-for-performance is pay-for-knowledge. Pay-for-knowledge refers to a system in which pay is determined by the number of jobs an employee can do, not by the job the employee actually does on any specific day. This type of system is seen more often in fast-food establishments, which use a team or crew concept.

REGULAR JOB EVALUATION AND ADVANCEMENT

Performance appraisal, the periodic evaluation of an employee's job performance, is one of the more negatively viewed and poorly performed of managerial tasks. Ron Zemke of *Training* magazine states: "Performance appraisals are about as beloved as IRS audits"

(Zemke, 1985). The term itself implies that the employer is scrutinizing the weaknesses of the employee. "Evaluation of employees," on the other hand, means much more simply a once-a-year performance appraisal. Evaluation is a managerial function and a responsibility that is critical to motivating employees and improving their performance and productivity. Regular performance evaluation is the key to utilizing and developing employees and involves on-going observation, assessment, documentation, and coaching of employees.

Coaching is a two-step process. First, job performance is analyzed. Second, performance is reinforced or corrected in a face-to-face situation. Coaching is a continual process during which the results of training and also the progress toward goals set in performance evaluation sessions are checked.

Some Coaching Tips

- Be a coach, not a drill sergeant. Do not stay constantly on employees' backs, watching or criticizing everything they do. The purpose of coaching is to help employees grow and improve their job performance. Being friendly and using praise does wonders
- When analyzing someone's job performance, if there appear to be problems, find out the possible causes. Be sure to discuss the situation with the employee. Does the employee know — and understand clearly — what to do? Does the employee know his or her performance is not satisfactory? Ask the employee questions, preferably open-ended ones, in an effort to help, not punish.
- When job performance is found to be in need of correction, first obtain agreement from the employee that a problem exists. Next, discuss together some possible solutions and mutually agree on a course of action to correct the concern. Follow-up is, of course, necessary. Recognize achievement.
- Listen to the employee during the coaching session. Be supportive and helpful.
- Correct errors promptly and in private. Employees are very sensitive about being told in front of their peers that they are doing something wrong. Unless the error could have grave consequences, wait to pull the employee aside to tell him or her how to correct the error.
- Recognize when an employee has reached his or her potential.

In addition to regular job evaluation, advancement opportunities may sell a job. Any employer can set up a career ladder in which an employee can be promoted by steps to higher level jobs, each requiring more skills and responsibility. Generally the progression of jobs is

Fig. 4-1 SAMPLE CAREER LADDER

evident by looking at the chain of command. For instance, in a fast-food restaurant, a crew member may aspire to become an assistant manager and then the unit manager. In a full-service restaurant, a bus person may work up to be a server and then on to a dining room supervisor and eventually a management trainee.

For a career ladder to work, the following need to be done.

1. Set up the career ladder. A good source for this will be your organizational chart. You may want to have a career ladder for all staff or one for just a part of the company, such as the cooking area. See Fig. 4-1 for an example.
2. Management needs to clearly set criteria for promotion. Criteria may include a minimum level of performance on past evaluations and a minimum amount of time on the current job. Criteria should be identified and communicated to all employees along with a promote-from-within policy statement.
3. Management must be completely committed in words and actions to it and must make it a long-term investment. Of course, within any business there are times when hiring an outsider is more desirable than promoting from within, such as when it is felt that a new perspective and ideas are needed. In such a case, it is important to communicate this to employees who did not get promoted.
4. Promotion procedures and standards must be adhered to consistently at all times. If they are relaxed for any individual, the credibility of the program will falter.
5. Employees must be promoted in a consistent and fair manner. Favoritism has no place in promotions.
6. When employees are promoted, provide tangible rewards and increased pay. Again, be consistent with your rewards and salary increases.

7. Do not be surprised or disappointed when someone who has been promoted does not work out. This will happen from time to time and does not necessarily mean the system is not working.
8. It is important to recognize that not everyone wants to be promoted or is promotable. Pressure should not be put on someone who is happy where he or she is.

EMPLOYEE REWARDS

Reward systems can be used to increase employee motivation and commitment. Traditional employee rewards include compensation and benefits (as discussed), safe and comfortable working conditions, and recognition for a job well done.

Examples of foodservice recognition programs include those used by Domino's Pizza and Pizza Hut. Both bring award winners to national meetings to praise their achievements. Some restaurants use sales figures, cover counts, and simple managerial judgment to give bonuses to employees in almost all job categories. For example, if the number of meals served in the dining room surpasses a certain number, the kitchen staff will receive a bonus; servers who exceed the average sales for a shift also receive bonuses. Other areas that can be acknowledged in recognition programs include good attendance, length of service, safety, training, quality of service, and teamwork.

National surveys from the 1980s have shown that traditional reward systems were not being perceived as rewarding by the majority of people at work (National Restaurant Association, 1987). In addition, most employees saw little connection between their pay and performance and felt that if productivity increased, they would not benefit. Lastly, most companies were not involving their employees very much. In a survey conducted by The American Productivity Center/American Compensation Association in 1986, the majority of organizations reported that their recognition programs had little impact on performance.

Nontraditional reward systems have been growing in use and, according to the survey just mentioned, are reported to impact positively on performance. Some of these are

Gain-sharing plans
Pay-for-performance
Business information sharing with employees
Employee participation programs
Emphasis on teamwork

Employers implementing reward systems should keep in mind that these programs work best when employees do not compete with each other. Recognition programs which reward only certain individuals do little to motivate employees and actually discourage many employees from taking part.

A late 1980s Gallup poll of a cross-section of employees from different industries showed that "84 percent of the interviewed employees said they would work harder and do a better job if they were involved in decisions affecting their work" (Denton, 1987). Potential benefits of participative management include higher productivity, improved morale, and better decisions. Participative managers share responsibility with those who perform the work, although, of course, the manager always assumes ultimate responsibility.

In order for participation to succeed, certain conditions need to be considered. What is selected for the employees to participate in must be relevant and of interest to the employees, and they should be able to communicate adequately with one another. Neither the manager nor the employees should feel that participation threatens the position of either. Employees need to feel that they can freely give opinions and suggestions, without any negative consequences. The possible benefits of participation should be greater than its costs, especially including the time commitment.

There are many kinds of employee participation programs, such as consultive management, work committees or quality circles, suggestion programs, employee ownership or profit-sharing plans, and team building. Consultive management occurs when managers consult with employees and ask them to think about and contribute ideas on certain situations before management makes a decision. This consultation is done informally.

Work committees, also known as quality circles, involve groups of workers who meet regularly on company time to identify and analyze job problems and develop possible solutions, which then go to management for evaluation and implementation. The problems may concern quality, productivity, safety, job structure, or work conditions. Groups usually consist of eight to ten employees from the same work area. Groups often choose their own leader to facilitate discussions or have a supervisory person do so. The leader needs formal training in working with such groups. Quality circles can work well, because employees who can generate their own solutions take ownership of them and are much more likely to support and implement them.

Suggestion programs are formal programs in which employees are asked to write down or otherwise express any suggestions they have to improve work methods or any other aspect of their job. A response rate in a suggestion program is typically about 15 percent, of which about one-quarter of the responses are implemented. Suggestion programs very often revolve around topics such as how to save money in an area or how to reduce accidents.

Worker participation programs will not succeed if the organization does not fully support them. Sure ways to kill these programs include poor managerial responses to employee suggestions, managers who are not trained to facilitate group discussions, insufficient time commitment, and no incentives for employees to contribute suggestions.

TRAINING AND ORIENTATION PROGRAMS AND MANUALS

A National Restaurant Association study of what the foodservice industry will look like in the year 2000 concluded that the industry will have to meet an increased need to train and develop its employees (National Restaurant Association, 1988). In the hospitality industry as a whole, unfortunately, training is a neglected function. Training requires a time commitment, which is tough to find in a business in which there is so much time pressure. Yet a good training program can both attract new employees and retain current ones, in part because training gives the employee a dual message: "You are important to this organization, and we care about how you do your job."

One example of a successful training program can be found in Hardee's "Served with Pride" program, which consists of seven modules: Sales and Service, Hospitality, Burgers, Deep Fry, Biscuits, Specialty Products, and Salads. Each module includes instructional videotapes and printed materials. All entry-level crew members must be certified in the Hospitality module, and certification in four or more of the modules is required for 80 percent of the crew members at each restaurant. There are also training modules developed for use by managers. The overall purpose of the program is to provide consistent and high-quality food and service. Hardee's training programs have been very well received by both hourly employees and management.

Chapter 9 contains some how-tos on training. In addition, in the appendix there can be found resources for obtaining or developing training programs, or both, and a checklist for developing a training program. Chapter 9 contains orientation information, including a new employee orientation checklist.

RELOCATION ASSISTANCE

When a new (or current) employee must move to take a new job, offering to pay part or all of the moving expenses may act as a real incentive. Some companies also pay, or help pay, the cost of traveling to the new area and sometimes some bills incurred from looking for a new place to live.

TRANSPORTATION ASSISTANCE

Companies may offer transportation assistance, which may take the form of offering reduced fare transit passes for employees in an urban area, organizing a car pool, or actually operating a company vehicle to bring employees to and from work.

CHILD-CARE ASSISTANCE

The percentage of working mothers with children under 6 years of age increased from 47 percent in the mid-1980s to 56 percent in 1988. In addition to the growing number of mothers in the work force, the number of women in childbearing years is projected to increase by 12 percent from 1988 to the year 2000 (Gordon, 1990). The issue of child care is particularly important for foodservice operators, because in 1988 females made up about 60 percent of hourly employees and 40 percent of salaried employees. Of even more importance is the fact that 40 percent of employees in foodservice are females in their childbearing years, ages 18 to 44 (National Restaurant Association, 1990).

In a 1989 nationwide survey by the Gallup Organization and the Employee Benefit Research Institute, 71 percent of respondents said that employers should do something to provide adequate child care (Gordon, 1990). Child-care assistance helps to meet the need of mothers in the work force for affordable child care while they work. It may be accomplished in many different ways:

On-site (or near-site) day-care facilities
Voucher or direct subsidies for off-site facilities
Employee reimbursement for all or part of child-care costs
Child-care services referral
Flexible spending accounts
Sick child care infirmary or in-home nursing service for children

Although employees most often prefer an on-site (or near-site) day-care facility, this option has difficulties. Two concerns with running this type of day-care facility are the legal liability issues and its cost.

On the other hand, implementing flexible spending accounts helps the employee and actually costs the employer little or nothing. With such an account, the employee designates a certain percentage of her salary for the employer to apply to child care. The employee is exempt from paying taxes on that portion of earnings, and the employer is also exempt from paying the Social Security tax on them as well. In this manner, the cost of establishing and administering the account is more than offset by the Social Security tax savings.

In a Bureau of Labor Statistics study conducted in 1987 among 10,000 businesses and government agencies that had at least ten employees, approximately 11 percent provided some employees with child-care assistance. In a 1989 National Restaurant Association survey, less than 2 percent of those surveyed subsidized any child-care expenses for salaried or hourly employees, or both. When employees did receive child-care assistance, they were eligible to receive it immediately and in most cases they were not required to work a minimum number of hours to receive it. Almost all employers reported providing flexible work schedules and time off for a sick child (Gordon, 1990).

Although foodservice operators have not been as quick to embrace the idea of child-care assistance, some operators are trying it out. For example, Marriott is working on offering on-site child care at its health-care, business and industry, and education accounts, by joining Corporate Child Care Inc., a provider of employer-sponsored day care, in a joint venture.

Books which give help in setting up some type of child-care assistance program are listed in the appendix.

SIGN-ON BONUS

Used most commonly as an incentive to attract salaried employees, sign-on bonuses represent a one-time payment to new hires. Sign-on bonuses are sometimes also used to make up for a salary which may not be quite as high as the applicant would like.

FLEXIBLE HOURS

Flexible hours are commonly offered to new employees. Instead of always working a specific set of hours, flexible hours are commonly an option. This is particularly attractive to employees who attend school, work at another job, or have children to care for.

ALTERNATIVE SCHEDULES

Some alternative scheduling ideas include flextime, job sharing, and compressed work schedules. They are more appropriate for managerial and clerical employees than for most hourly foodservice workers.

The concept of flextime involves all employees being at work during core hours, such as 9:00 A.M. to 4:00 P.M. for secretaries. They then choose which time they arrive and depart from work. The actual arrangements vary from company to company. Although this type of arrangement requires more supervision, it also may increase employee job satisfaction, morale, and performance, as the employee has more control over his or her time.

In job sharing, a single full-time job is filled or shared by two part-time individuals. Typically, they work at different times but often have an overlap of work hours to coordinate their work. It is important to lay out exactly what each person will be doing and who will be responsible for each job duty. It is also important that the two employees be compatible and have similar work standards. Although this type of arrangement does not sound too easy, it has reportedly worked quite well.

Job sharing does often cost more, but there are also benefits to this arrangement. When one person is out due to vacation, and so on, the other can step in. Likewise, if things are really hectic, more help is available without resorting to overtime. When one of the two people leaves the job, the other is there to train the newcomer. Part-timers also tend to be more efficient with their time. Since job-sharing employees are frequently mothers who have children at home or in school, it makes more sense to offer job sharing than to lose a good employee.

Compressed work schedules involve working a full-time schedule in less than 40 scheduled hours. Such a schedule usually involves working four 10-hour work days. It is beneficial from the perspective of reduced absenteeism and burnout as well as better employee morale.

PARENTAL LEAVE

Some companies offer time off to women or men when a child is born or adopted. Partial or full pay and benefits may be granted as well. Other types of personal leave may be granted to care for an ill parent or for other family emergencies.

TUITION REIMBURSEMENT

For many employees in the 18 to 24 age group, tuition reimbursement can be a valuable incentive, as many of them do want to obtain an education. Examples of successful programs include the following.

- Au Bon Pain, a fast-food chain, offers to employees who have worked at least 750 hours either a $1,000 scholarship or a $500 bonus.
- Chick-fil-A, another fast-food chain, offers scholarships to crew members who have worked for at least 2 years.
- Burger King allows employees to build up to $2,000 of tuition credits in 2 years starting after an employee has been on board for 3 months. The program is financed by each unit and works like the G.I. Bill.

Another method was used by an owner and operator of two Burger Kings in Detroit who worked with local community colleges to begin an educational incentive program. Based upon the number of hours worked per week, tuition and books were paid for one, two, or three courses. The more hours worked, the more courses would be paid. No prerequisite work experience was required, and the employee was required only to meet with a counselor at the college for advice when registering for courses. In an 8-month study, results showed a 39-percent turnover rate for employees who used the program, as compared with a 160 percent turnover rate for employees who did not take advantage of the program. The turnover rate for high school students was 118 percent.

FREE UNIFORMS OR UNIFORM ALLOWANCE

Free uniforms, especially if they are also laundered, are another incentive. If this is not possible, each employee could be allowed a certain amount of money each year for uniform replacement. In this manner, the employer does not have to purchase new uniforms or maintain stock, and there are none of the inconveniences of providing uniforms.

FREE MEALS OR MEAL ALLOWANCE

Mealtime for foodservice employees is just as important as for employees in other industries, and free, or partially subsidized, meals are welcomed by virtually all new employees.

5

Internal Recruiting

Internal recruiting methods range from very informal, such as a manager filling an assistant manager position with a promising employee, to more formal and clearly laid out methods, such as job posting and succession plans. Internal recruiting also includes employee referral programs, a practice which became very popular during the 1980s. This chapter will discuss and give guidelines for each internal recruiting method.

Job Posting

Job posting is the practice of advertising open positions within the foodservice operation to current employees. This is usually accomplished by making lists of open positions available to employees or posting these lists on bulletin boards which are often designated for this purpose, or both (see Fig. 5-1). In many instances, the positions are offered to present employees before recruiting from the outside occurs. Employees must then respond within a certain number of days after the job has been posted.

Guidelines for Posting Jobs

- You may want to set up stipulations for employees who want to respond to a job posting. For example, you may require that the employee be with the company for at least one year, in his or her

Fig. 5-1 JOB POSTING

JOB POSTING

Date: Friday, June 3, 1990
Department: Kitchen
Job Title: Cook
Grade: 8
Hours: 9:00 A.M.—5:00 P.M.

JOB QUALIFICATIONS
Knowledge: Has knowledge of cooking terminology and ingredents

Skills and Abilities: Measures; uses a knife; identifies and uses various pieces of small and large kitchen equipment; reads and follows recipes; does basic math (addition, subtraction, multiplication, and division); uses any cooking method; determines degree of doneness in cooked foods; uses portion control tools; garnishes; works well with others

Work Experience: One year of satisfactory experience as a cook required; two to three years cooking experience preparing a variety of menu items preferred

Education and Training: Culinary training preferred

Department: Dining Room
Job Title: Server
Grade: 6
Hours: 4:30 P.M.—10:30 P.M.

Fig. 5-1 Continued

JOB QUALIFICATIONS
Knowledge: <u>Has basic knowledge of food and cooking</u>

Skills and Abilities: <u>Presents a good appearance; is neat and</u>
<u>well groomed; interacts with guests in a courteous and</u>
<u>helpful manner; works well with other personnel; writes</u>
<u>neatly; performs basic mathematical functions (addition,</u>
<u>subtraction, multiplication, and division); sets tables;</u>
<u>serves and clears</u>

Work Experience: <u>Six months satisfactory experience as a</u>
<u>server required; one year preferred</u>

Education and Training: <u>High school diploma or service</u>
<u>training, or both, preferred</u>

If you have been in your current position at least 90 days with a
satisfactory evaluation and you think you meet the job qualifications, you
must come to the personnel office by <u>Friday, June 10, 1990</u> *to*
apply for any position posted.

job for at least 6 months, and have a satisfactory or better rating on the most recent performance evaluation. These types of rules help prevent excessive job hopping.

- Post open positions where they are most likely to be seen and read.
- For each job posting, include the following information: department, exemption status, salary grade and range, hours of work, job qualifications, and the deadline for applying.
- Post open positions for a certain period of time, such as three days, before offering the job to an outside candidate.
- Treat in-house applicants the same or better than outside applicants.
- Make sure in-house applicants are told as soon as possible whether or not they have gotten the position so they do not hear about it through the grapevine.
- Be honest with them about the reasons they did not get the position. If they lacked the qualifications to do the job, help them become qualified so they can reapply when an opening occurs again.

Employee Data Bank

Some companies maintain a computerized data base of employee skills, which they use in place of, or in addition to, job posting. This system may be developed in-house or done by an outside firm. If it is done in-house, computer hardware and software will be required. When a position becomes open, the computer generates a list of current employees who might be able to fill the position. It is imperative to keep a system such as this up to date.

Succession Plans

Succession plans are found at the upper levels of management within medium to large companies and are typically developed by a committee of appropriate managers. First, the committee forecasts the short- and long-term staffing needs of the company in their upper-echelon jobs and identifies the positions from which people can be promoted. Once these steps are taken, for each job forecasted the committee will identify two or three candidates who are promotable to these positions. These candidates are then trained so that they can obtain the skills and experience they will need in the event they are promoted.

Someone is usually assigned to oversee this, and a deadline for obtaining the skills and experience is set.

The succession plan is reviewed periodically, for example, once or twice a year, to check that there are still enough candidates for each position and that the training is going along properly. Typically, a program like this is kept confidential within the company. When such a program is not kept confidential, it may cause poor morale and performance by those employees who are not considered promotable.

Employee Referral Programs

Employee referral programs involve a current employee referring an applicant to the company who is then hired through the normal selection process. Usually a cash or merchandise reward is given to the employee who refers an applicant who is hired. Actual rewards vary, from a 10-cent hourly raise to a $250 cash bonus, radios, tickets to sports events, or points toward merchandise. Often the program is limited to certain positions which are the hardest to fill or require special skills, or both. These programs have been used very successfully by some companies to draw in new workers and to improve morale.

Guidelines for Employee Referral Programs

- Make it an on-going program. If you have any specific recruitment campaigns of limited duration, be sure to publicize the deadlines widely.
- Make sure all employees are aware of the program through posters, meetings, and notices in their paycheck envelopes. List on these materials why your company is such a great place to work. Be certain to inform employees of any change in the program.
- Include all employees in the program, with one exception. A manager or a supervisor should not be eligible for a referral if the person in the position reports to him or her. Make sure the program guidelines are being applied consistently.
- A referral form or card (see Fig. 5-2) should be filled out by the employee who is referring the applicant. You may want the employee to hand this in at the same time that the applicant hands in the application.
- The referral reward need not be extravagant. It should be of appropriate value and desirable to your employees.
- The referral reward should be based on the scarity of job appli-

Fig. 5-2   EMPLOYEE REFERRAL FORM

EMPLOYEE REFERRAL PROGRAM
REFERRAL FORM

Date: _____

Employee's Name: _____

Name of Applicant You Are Referring: _____

Name of Position(s) Desired: _____

Days and Hours Available for Work: _____

Please attach an Employee Application Form completed by your referral. If the applicant meets the minimum qualifications, he or she will be contacted shortly to come in for an interview. Applicants referred to Personnel through the Employee Referral Program are given the same consideration as other applicants.

cants for the position and not on the level of the position within the foodservice.

- Set a period of time for the new employee to work before the referring employee receives either the entire reward or, if part of the award was already given, the remaining portion of the award. It is a good idea to wait until the probationary period has been completed, which is, in most cases, from 60 to 90 days.
- To increase participation, hold drawings of all referring employees and give away grand prizes.

Other Internal Recruiting Methods

Other ways to recruit include checking the files for previous applicants and speaking with walk-in, call-in, or write-in applicants. Checking previously submitted applications unfortunately often yields poor results, as the good applicants have likely found other jobs. With regard to people who come in person to apply for a job, be sure they fill out an employment application. If an interview cannot be done at that moment, be sure to schedule one. When appropriate, call-in and write-in candidates should be asked to fill in applications.

6

External Recruiting

In this chapter we discuss external recruiting methods, such as advertising. Specific recruiting groups, such as college students and the handicapped, and methods to reach each of them also will be examined.

Most external recruiting methods fall into one of four categories: advertising; using an employment service; contacting outside referral sources, such as schools; and special events, such as job fairs.

Advertising

Advertising means much more than simply placing an ad in the Sunday paper. In addition to newspapers, advertisements can appear in magazines and publications of professional and trade associations, as well as on television, radio, and billboards. Direct mail is another form of advertising. Many companies are spending more money on advertising due to the intense competition for employees. For example, display advertisements using the company's logo are more common and also more attention-getting than the traditional classified advertisements, which are smaller and less costly.

When placing job ads, you need to consider both what to say and where and when to place the ad. Regardless of the type of ad, it should include the following basic information:

Company name
Information about the company
Position title, requirements, and responsibilities
How to apply (by sending a resume, calling, or applying in person)

Information that can be used to help sell the job includes competitive pay, a complete benefits package, free meals, training, flexible work hours, or the opportunity for advancement as appropriate. All information should be clearly stated. The ad must convey the feeling that the company is stable and secure.

Whether it is for a display or a classified ad, grab the readers' attention with an ad that is eye-catching and quick and easy to read. Varying the size and boldness of print as well as having some white space makes the content easier to read. When possible, use a company logo, as it often attracts the reader's attention and also builds your company's image.

Other Strategies for Developing Display Ads

- Use power words in headlines to attract attention. For example, one restaurant chain used fanciful, job-induced ailments in their headlines to attract managers who felt a lack of growth in their current jobs (Fig. 6-1). Other headlines that were used described "promisphobia — the fear of joining a company whose promises never pan out" and "letdownitis — the deflated feeling when your company's growth doesn't match your career ambitions." The use of these one-word headlines and clever definitions did bring in many more applicants.
- Give readers a way to respond easily to the ad. This can be done by asking readers to fill in mini-resumes, postcard questionnaires, or simply response cards.
- Depict a success story about an employee in your company who moved up the ranks.

When you are writing recruiting advertisements, be careful to avoid gender-specific references, such as waiter, busboy, or hostess. These are discriminatory and therefore illegal. Preferable terms would be "server," "bus person," and "host/hostess." Also, avoid age-specific references, such as "young" or "recent college graduate."

When you are choosing a newspaper, it is important that you examine and compare the area where it is distributed, its circulation, characteristics of the readership, and advertising rates. This information can be obtained by talking with people in the circulation and advertising departments. They can also give you information about

Fig. 6-1 DISPLAY ADVERTISEMENT

Source: Reprinted with permission of Buffets, Inc.

special sections in which your ads may run. They can also tell you if they publish other publications, in which case you can usually get better rates if you advertise in more than one newspaper or magazine, or both.

Circulation and readership information is also important when implementing an affirmative action plan because you need to target your advertisements to media that are most frequently used by the labor groups you want to reach. For example, if Hispanics are a targeted labor group, you will want to put ads into Spanish language newspapers or on Spanish language radio stations.

Sunday is often the best day of the week on which to advertise. Avoid advertising on holiday weekends, as the classified section is quite thin and the ads do not do as well.

Although most job ads go into a classified section, this need not always be the case. Display ads can also be placed in the food section of newspapers and magazines.

You may choose to use an advertising agency which can help you write, design, and place ads. Agencies can be particularly helpful in laying out an ad in terms of size and boldness of letters, spacing, and placement of artwork.

Guidelines for Selecting an Advertising Agency

- Does the agency have experience doing ads for foodservices?
- What other accounts does the agency handle?
- How well have some of the agency's recent ads done? Ask to look at them.
- Does it have a good working relationship with and knowledge of the media?
- Who would handle your account?
- What is its ability in preparing recruiting strategies?
- How quickly can it put together what you need?
- Has the agency won any advertising awards?
- What is its billing procedure?
- Does the agency seem interested in your project?

Blind advertisements do not identify the employer and use a box number for responses. This type of advertisement generally gets a lower rate of response and should therefore be avoided unless necessary. Readers wonder who the company is (it could even be their current employer) and are discouraged from applying. They are useful, for instance, when a manager resigns and you want to fill the position but do not want anyone in-house to know the manager is leaving.

Advertising can also be done on radio and television, which are excellent media to reach a large number of people. Unfortunately, the cost is very high, in part because the message must be repeated many times to be effective. In addition, the services of an advertising agency are usually needed. If you use radio or television advertising to reach a specific group, such as teenagers, be sure to feature them in the ad. Lastly, local cable stations have more reasonable rates than network television stations.

Direct mail is a form of advertising which is not used too often but can at times be effective. From your area Chamber of Commerce you can get a list of area newcomers to whom you may want to mail a packet of coupons, menu, or employment information, or all of these. This could also be done through "Welcome Wagon" or another organization which welcomes newcomers.

Open positions can be publicized at low cost within your operation, for instance, on place mats, receipts, table tents, bag stuffers, and indoor or outdoor signs. If you offer home delivery or take-out, make sure an employment flier goes out with orders. One sure way to attract attention and to get applicants is to have response cards available to customers which they can fill out quickly and leave for employment consideration. The front of the card uses headlines and copy to entice customers to fill out the back of the card, which is like a mini-application. The idea is to make it easy for people to fill it in quickly and hand in.

Open positions can also be publicized at low cost by posting notices in health clubs, libraries, supermarkets, synagogues, churches, community centers, and a YMCA or a YWCA.

Employment Services

PRIVATE EMPLOYMENT AGENCIES

Private employment agencies vary greatly in size of business and quality of services provided. Normally they charge a fee to the employer, which the agency does not collect until an applicant they send has been selected and hired. Often, if a newly placed employee leaves the job during a specified period of time, referred to as the "guarantee period," the agency must find a suitable replacement or return the fee. The amount of the fee is based on a percentage of the employee's salary, although fees are often negotiable. In 44 states, private employment agencies are regulated by laws that limit how much they can charge as a fee for service.

When you are looking for an employment agency, ask the following questions:

Does the agency handle any other foodservice companies?
What is its track record in placing candidates who stay at least 3 months, or preferably 1 year?
Will the agency provide references? How do their other clients rate their services?
How will the agency screen and interview applicants?
What will be the fee arrangement? Will this be put in writing?
Who will be handling your account?

Be sure to call references and check up on the agency's reputation and ability to do its job.

Private agencies prefer, of course, to be used exclusively during a job search; however, if they are not providing good results, it is best to ask another agency for applicants as well.

Once an employment agency has been chosen, use these guidelines to get the best results. Remember that the more an agency knows about you and your operation, the better they can do their job.

Guidelines for Using an Employment Agency

- Offer to show your operation to the agency.
- Thoroughly describe your recruiting requirements. Give the agency appropriate job descriptions and minimum requirements for applicants so they can effectively screen people.
- Verify in writing the fee structure and refund policy. A typical refund policy states that 90 percent of the fee will be returned if the employee stays less than 30 days, 60 percent will be returned if the employee stays from 30 to 60 days, and 30 percent will be returned if the employee stays from 60 to 90 days.
- It is better to work closely with a small number of agencies and build a good business relationship than to work with many different agencies.
- Check with the agency to see if it will advertise the position.

TEMPORARY AGENCIES

During the 1980s, temporary agencies grew in size and importance. Although once thought of mostly as a source for vacation relief and clerical help, these agencies can supply much more than that. There are even a small number of temporary agencies specializing in filling positions for hotels, restaurants, and caterers. Many agencies can provide foodservice employees who will stay for as little as a day or as long as they are needed. For example, Uniforce is a national company which places food production, as well as industrial and clerical, personnel.

Temporary agencies charge by the hour. Although their hourly rates are from 50 to 150 percent higher than a typical salary for the position, this will be partially or completely offset because employee benefits, such as health benefits, paid time off, Social Security and workers' compensation, do not have to be paid. The higher rate covers the agency's overhead and profit, of course. The agency may pay workers' compensation, benefits, and liability insurance for its employees.

The advantage of using temporary agency employees is that they can help, for instance, during peak business periods or when a regular employee is out due to vacation, sickness, and so on. Temporary agencies seem most able to provide emergency fill-in personnel and entry-level workers.

On the other hand, a disadvantage is that the employer must spend varying amounts of time and money to train temporary employees, who then will leave. Also, it is not uncommon to see a lack of consistency in job performance, perhaps in part because the temporary employee lacks commitment to a job that he or she will be leaving soon. One way to counteract this problem is to treat the temporary employee exactly as a regular employee in terms of orientation and training.

The best way to examine a temporary agency is to make a visit in person.

Guidelines for Evaluating a Temporary Agency

- Check on the number of full-time staff members and the agency's financial stability.
- Ask how applicants are recruited.
- Find out how the agency screens applications and interviews, tests, and checks references on applicants.
- Ask how the agency trains foodservice employees, and look at any training manuals or materials.
- Ask if the employees are bonded, so that you will be insured against any losses caused by them.
- Check to see if the agency's employees are covered by liability insurance (and how much) or by workers' compensation. If the agency cannot provide a certificate to prove that workers' compensation is provided, you will have to provide it.
- Find out if the agency has filled similar positions in other foodservices in the area. Get the names of other companies, and ask them if they were pleased with the ability of the temporary employees to do their jobs and to fit into the work environment.
- Ask how the agency will follow up on temporary employees who will be assigned to you. Ask if there is a money-back or exchange guarantee if the temporary employees do not work out.

By getting answers to these questions ahead of time, you can avoid incurring many problems later.

EXECUTIVE SEARCH FIRMS

Executive search firms are used to fill upper-level management positions. Although they operate in essence like employment agencies, executive search firms act quite differently (see Table 6-1), and they are not subject to state regulations governing employment agencies. These firms are paid by their clients for time and expenses, even if the client does not choose one of their candidates. Typically, the fee is

Table 6-1 Differences Between Employment Agencies and Executive Search Firms

	Employment Agencies	Executive Search Firms
Fees	Range from 10 to 35% of starting salary. Paid only when position has been filled.	Range from 30 to 35% of starting salary. Paid in installments. Must be paid even if the position has been filled by other means.
Positions handled	Often fill lower-level and entry-level positions.	Fill middle- and upper-management positions.
How positions are filled	Information on positions to be filled often given on telephone. Agents work on filling many positions at a time. Recruit applicants who are actively seeking jobs. Send many applicants to client.	Consultant researches client's company and position requirements. Consultant works on from three to six open positions at a time. Recruit applicants who usually are not seeking employment. Send smaller number of more qualified applicants.

paid in three installments: in advance, during the search, and when the job has been filled.

The professional standards and activities of executive search firms are regulated by two trade groups. The Association of Executive Search Consultants includes only consulting firms. The National Association of Corporate and Professional Recruiters includes management consultants and their corporate clients.

Following are questions to ask other clients of the search firm.

Is the search firm well respected by other past or present clients?

For what percentage of clients has it successfully completed a search?

Does the search firm deliver qualified candidates in a timely manner from the designated geographical area?

How much does the firm do to understand an organization and its
needs? Does it have experience in the foodservice industry?

Does the search firm assign a search consultant who is compatible
and works well with others in the organization?

Does the search firm keep the organization well informed as to the
progress being made?

Does the search firm successfully maintain confidentiality?

What type of written contract is provided?

U.S. EMPLOYMENT SERVICE

In addition to private employment agencies, there is the U.S. Employment Service, which is a federal and state system of employment offices referred to as Job Service Centers or Offices. The nearest Job Service Office can be located in the telephone directory under Job Service, Employment Service, or Employment Security Commission. These agencies do not charge a fee and will screen and provide applicants typically for entry-level jobs.

Referrals from Job Service Centers are unemployed and therefore can usually start work immediately if hired. One concern with the public employment agencies is that they do at times send unqualified applicants. When this happens, be sure to provide clear documentation that the individual did not meet the job qualifications.

Job Service Centers can also give you information about apprenticeship programs. Apprenticeship programs include both on-the-job and classroom training. For example, chef apprenticeship programs can be found in community colleges. These programs must meet federally approved standards.

LEASING COMPANIES

The concept of leasing companies is new. Leasing companies are used as a source of employees on a long-term basis. Typically, these companies hire employees who are then trained and leased to the foodservice company. The leasing company essentially acts as the human resource department for the foodservice company by taking over the function of staffing and payroll in return for a service fee. Employees often like working for leasing companies because they frequently get better benefits and more variety in their jobs. One Chicago leasing company reports saving restaurants about 2 percent of their gross payroll.

Outside Referral Sources

PROFESSIONAL ASSOCIATIONS AND SOCIETIES

Many professional associations and societies publish "Help Wanted" advertisements in their publications on a regular basis.

STUDENTS

College or university students represent an excellent source of job applicants, particularly if they are enrolled in a foodservice management, culinary, or hotel, restaurant, and institution management curriculum. For best long-term results, efforts should be concentrated on building and maintaining a lasting relationship with the college or university. Also, do not limit yourself to hospitality students when you are recruiting. Students with liberal arts or business majors, such as accounting, may choose to select a career in foodservice.

Strategies for Reaching Students

- Contact the job placement office. In addition to posting your open positions, a job placement coordinator can help you set up interviews with graduating students.
- Contact the person(s) running the foodservice program or business program, or both. Work on developing a professional relationship with that person.
- Have available some professionally designed and printed material on your organization, which includes information on your type of business and its work location(s), descriptions of available jobs, job qualifications, and career advancement possibilities. This often takes the form of a brochure, but recently some companies have developed their own videotapes, which have proved to be an excellent medium for conveying information.
- Offer to be a guest lecturer on specific topics in the foodservice curriculum.
- Invite classes to take a tour of your operation.
- Offer to take on students for internship/externship, co-operative, and summer work assignments, as well as apprenticeship programs.
- Offer to take part in a job fair or a career day at the college.
- Invite educators to take a tour of your foodservice.
- Set up a scholarship fund.

- Offer to become a member of an advisory board.
- Provide summer jobs for faculty members.
- Donate any used equipment to the college's kitchen facility.
- Advertising can be done on college campuses through school newspapers, sporting events, bag stuffers at the bookstore, job-posting fliers, yearbooks, and club publications.

On-campus recruiting demands careful preparation, as recruiters may interview many students each day during relatively short interview periods.

In addition to recruiting current students, it is also advantageous to locate college graduates when possible through alumni associations. Some alumni associations have newsletters which can run information about job openings. A new trend among alumni associations has been to keep a data base of graduates which companies can then access for a fee. Typically, an employer gives a profile of the candidates desired and then receives names of people who match the profile and have agreed to have their names released.

High school and vocational/technical students also represent potential employees. You can recruit these students by

Posting job notices on bulletin boards
Teaching classes in home economics, cooking, or foodservice
Advertising in school newspapers and publications
Speaking during career days
Arranging through the Guidance Department to interview graduating students

FRATERNAL ORGANIZATIONS

Fraternal organizations such as the Elks, Girl and Boy Scouts, and church groups can also be contacted for recruiting purposes.

NETWORKING

Networking with other professionals, both within foodservice and outside the field, is vital. This can be done by attending meetings of professional organizations, such as state National Restaurant Association meetings, business associations such as the Chamber of Commerce or Rotary, and civic groups. Work on establishing a good relationship with all those who are good referral sources by inviting them for lunch or dinner and a tour, giving them printed brochures on your organization, and putting them on your mailing list for newsletters and press releases.

It is especially important to keep in touch with other area foodservice operators, because foodservice employees often work at both a full-time and a part-time job. Therefore, you may ask them if any of their employees are looking for a part-time job.

Special Events

JOB OR CAREER FAIR

At a job or career fair, usually one company sponsors the show and sells booths to other companies. The job fair can be scheduled to last one or several days and may sometimes be held on a weekend. Advertisements, typically in the newspaper, serve to attract candidates. Each company then brings recruiters, job information, company brochures, and pamphlets. Recruiters usually just screen candidates in a fairly brief interview to determine if a full interview at a later date would be beneficial. In this manner, the recruiter can see more candidates than if a full interview were conducted. Also, the physical environment usually does not offer a quiet, private location where an interview can take place.

OPEN HOUSE

Another type of special event is the open house. For this event, a company opens its doors to applicants, who are then interviewed by recruiters. Again, advertising is done and should include a listing of all available jobs. In some instances, applicants may be asked to submit resumes in advance as a way to determine what the turnout will be.

Recruiting Specific Groups

Appendix A contains addresses and telephone numbers for many of the organizations mentioned in this section.

MINORITIES

The U.S. Department of Labor forecasts that, within the next few years, 75 percent of those entering the work force will comprise minority members and women. For the first time, white males now make up only 46 percent of the work force. This trend will continue due to the combination of a declining, older white American population and a younger, growing minority population. Also, since 1988 immigration restrictions have eased, especially for individuals who can fill entry-level service jobs.

- Ask for assistance from the National Urban League and the National Association for the Advancement of Colored People. Both associations work at bringing blacks into the economic mainstream of American society through skill-training programs, counseling, and job placement services.
- Check on minority community agencies in your area.
- Contact ministers at minority churches.
- Run job ads in minority newspapers.
- Advertise in foreign-language newspapers.
- Post notices in youth centers and apartment buildings in ethnic neighborhoods.
- Speak to classes in schools in minority neighborhoods.
- Contact English as a Second Language classes in the public schools.

WOMEN

Women represent a valuable source of part-time employees because many of them have home and family obligations, which make part-time hours highly desirable. Also, part-time work provides income and the chance to interact with people. As an employer, do not forget that this group often needs flexibility with its working hours.

- Contact women's groups, such as Displaced Homemaker organizations and the National Organization of Women.
- Contact an agency for single parents.
- Post signs in child-care centers, supermarkets, and health clubs.
- Contact the U.S. Department of Labor (Employment and Training Administration) or the local private industry to inquire about women's training programs in your area.

SENIOR CITIZENS

Hiring retirees is becoming popular as this segment of the population grows. The over-65 group will increase to 20 percent of the population in 2020 from 12 percent in 1987. For each year from 1988 to 2000, the number of men aged 55 to 64 will increase 1.1 percent, and women of the same age, 1.8 percent. An industry example is

McDonald's McMasters program, in which persons who are older than 55 are offered jobs and training. Retirees often return to work to fight feelings of loneliness and boredom.

Retirees tend to be loyal, dependable, willing workers, and service-oriented. They come to work on time, have much prior work experience, and do their jobs well. Myths concerning older employees' problems with productivity, absenteeism, flexibility, and higher health insurance and training costs are just that—myths.

To the advantage of many foodservice operators, most senior citizens want to work part-time. Because most are receiving Social Security benefits, they do not want to work too many hours and earn too much money; otherwise, they would have to pay some money back into Social Security.

The number of retirees who do go back to work is actually quite small. Possible reasons why they do not return to work include higher tax rates, transportations costs, and possible penalties imposed on pension benefits. A Bureau of Labor Statistics study shows that there has been little increase in the proportion of older workers in foodservice between 1983 and 1988. It may actually be easier to retain current employees who are close to retirement by finding out and meeting their needs better so that they would consider working longer.

Following are various methods to use to recruit senior citizens. When you are recruiting this group, emphasize how much you value their experience, the social aspects of the job, the flexibility of the job, and the opportunity to help others.

- Contact the American Association for Retired Persons Senior Employment Services.
- Contact and post signs in senior citizen centers.
- Contact and post signs in retirement communities.
- Your local Chamber of Commerce and Agency on Aging can give you names of other groups in your area to contact.
- Offer tours to senior citizen groups.
- Contact the Senior Community Service Employment Programs found in every county. These agencies train senior citizens in needed skills and then help them find jobs.

DISABLED

A disabled or handicapped person is defined as someone who has a physical, mental, or developmental impairment that significantly limits one or more of life's major activities. A disabled person may be someone who is visually or hearing impaired; has a history of mental or emotional illness; has cerebral palsy, muscular dystrophy, or cardiovascular disease; or is a reformed alcoholic or drug abuser. Often a disabled person is mentally retarded.

According to the Vocational Rehabilitation Administration in Washington, D.C., approximately 18,000 people with disabilities are currently working in foodservice. There are many more who are able and willing to work in foodservice but cannot find employment. Approximately two-thirds of all handicapped people between the ages of 16 and 64 are not working, and two-thirds of this group would like to work.

Although it often takes longer to train them and their productivity is lower, handicapped employees tend to be dedicated, enthusiastic, hardworking, and reliable individuals who stay with their jobs. Disabled employees tend to value their jobs quite highly, in part because it was more of a struggle to get them in the first place. The mentally disabled person can do jobs such as cleaning and simple food preparation. The hearing-impaired person may be able to do cold food preparation or wash dishes and pots.

One company which has very successfully recruited and incorporated disabled employees into its staff since the 1960s is the Friendly Ice Cream Corporation, a chain of family restaurants. Working with local job service and rehabilitation agencies, it has recruited and trained about 1,600 disabled people to work in the company's 800 stores. Other companies which have made a point of hiring the disabled include the Marriott Corporation, McDonald's, Burger King, and Pizza Hut.

Guidelines for Recruiting Handicapped Individuals

- Contact your state or local vocational rehabilitation agency. It provides various services, such as vocational and on-the-job training, to disabled persons who can benefit from such training. Although the disabled often receive vocational training, the most effective training for them will be on-the-job training.
- Also contact your closest Job Service Center.
- Goodwill Industries of America, Inc., has many sites throughout the country with formal foodservice training and placement programs for the disabled.
- Contact the National Restaurant Association, Handicapped Employment Program Division.
- If there is a school for the deaf in your area, contact it.

When the disabled are hired, they may lose or receive reduced disability benefits. It is important to work out with job applicants ahead of time the number of hours they will work and the rate of pay they will receive.

VETERANS

Veterans represent yet another good source of foodservice employees. Retired military personnel have been recruited by various means. Sources to contact include the Veterans Administration and the local Veterans of Foreign Wars and American Legion. At the federal level, there are veterans employment and training programs. You can call the U.S. Department of Labor to get information about these programs in your area, or call your Job Service Center or Private Industry Council.

Federal Programs

The Job Training Partnership Act (JTPA), which replaced the old Comprehensive Employment and Training Act (CETA), was established to provide training for economically disadvantaged youths and adults, as well as displaced workers. Their programs are often coordinated with any of 600 local Private Industry Councils (PICs) and Job Service Offices. PICs are made up mostly of people from private industry, as well as representatives from labor unions and community-based organizations. They administer many government-funded services and programs on a local level. Businesses often contribute money toward job-training programs. Your nearest Job Service Office can be located by looking in the telephone directory under Job Service, Employment Service, Employment Security Commission, or the state government.

Apprenticeship programs include both on-the-job and classroom training. For example, chef apprenticeship programs can be found in some community colleges. These programs must meet federally approved standards, and in most cases the applicant must be at least 16 years old and have a high school diploma or GED. The federal standards are set by the Bureau of Apprenticeship and Training within the Department of Labor. There are also state apprenticeship and training councils within about 30 states.

The Targeted Jobs Tax Credit (TJTC) is a federal program which gives tax credits to businesses that hire hard-to-employ individuals, such as the disabled. It is underutilized by managers in the foodservice industry, despite the fact that it is actually not too time-consuming to operate. The rationale behind the program is to encourage employers to recruit, hire, and train individuals who are hard to employ, which often can be quite time-consuming. There are nine targeted groups in this program:

1. Vocational rehabilitation referrals
2. Economically disadvantaged youths from 18 to 22 years of age
3. Economically disadvantaged Vietnam War veterans
4. Supplemental Security Income recipients
5. General-assistance recipients
6. Economically disadvantaged cooperative education students from 16 to 19 years of age
7. Economically disadvantaged ex-convicts
8. Aid to Families with Dependent Children recipients and Work Incentive employees
9. Economically disadvantaged summer youth employees from 16 to 17 years of age

In order for the business to be eligible to use the TJTC, the employee must be certified by the local office of your state employment agency before the first day of employment. TJTC-eligible employees often do not want to go to get certified and may therefore require some prodding. Also, they may need to present proof of age and income when they go.

The TJTC credit is generally equal to 40 percent of up to $6,000 of qualified first-year wages for a maximum of $2,400 per employee. For economically disadvantaged summer youth employees, the credit is equal to 40 percent of up to $3,000 of wages for a maximum of $1,200. In addition to the financial benefit, some companies using TJTC report other benefits, such as feeling good about hiring those in need, increased company pride, and workers who are motivated and loyal. Because many TJTC-eligible workers have never had a paying job before, they are proud to be working and show much loyalty.

The TJTC program must be renewed yearly by the federal government so it is important to check on its current status.

THREE

Evaluating, Selecting, and Hiring

7

Evaluating
Applicants

The first step taken in evaluating applicants is usually asking them to fill out an application form. After the initial screening of the application, the applicant may go through further evaluation: interviewing, preemployment testing, and background checks. Because interviewing is so popular and complex, it is the subject of Chapter 8.

Keep in mind that no one method used to evaluate or measure applicants does a complete job. Each has its advantages and disadvantages. Keep in mind also that evaluation methods should be predictive of future job performance, should give consistent results, and should provide value for time and money spent.

Once an applicant has gone through the necessary parts of the evaluation process, a final selection decision can be made. This is the topic of Chapter 9.

Applications and Screening

Figure 7-1 is an example of an application form. Applications are used by almost all organizations. Basic information obtained on an application form includes name and address, previous work experience, education, references, and miscellaneous information. Some companies have one application for exempt jobs and a separate application for nonexempt jobs; each of which asks for slightly different information.

Based mostly on EEO laws, information requested on applications

Fig. 7-1 SAMPLE EMPLOYMENT APPLICATION

Personnel Management **Application For Employment**	**Date**
	Month Day Year

Equal Opportunity/Affirmative Action Employer

The company will not discriminate against an applicant or employee because of race, sex, age, religious creed, political affiliation, national origin, sexual preference, handicap, or any veteran status.

Last Name First Middle Initial	Social Security Number
Present address (Street & Number) City State ZIP Code	Home Phone Number
Address where you may be contacted if different from present address	Alternate Phone Number

Are you 18 years of age   U.S. Citizen or Resident Alien?   If no, indicate type of visa
or older? _____   ☐YES ☐NO

JOB INTEREST

Position you are applying for:	Type of position you eventually desire:

Occupational Objective

_____

_____

_____

Applying for ☐Full time Weekends ☐Yes ☐No ☐Part Time	Part Time Hours Desired:

When would you be available to begin work?

Have you previously been employed by us?   Previous Position(s) with this Company
☐Yes   ☐No   If yes, when?

How were you referred to this company?
☐Advertisement ☐Employee Referral ☐Employment Agency ☐Your Own Initiative ☐Other

Other than traffic violations and summary offenses, have you ever been convicted of a crime? If yes, what was it for, when did it happen, and what type of rehabilitation have you had?

Physical Record: Do you possess any physical disabilities which would prevent you from performing the duties required in the position sought?
☐Yes   ☐No

Give Details: _____

_____

PERSON TO BE NOTIFIED IN CASE OF EMERGENCY

Name	Phone Number
Address	

Fig. 7-1 Continued

EDUCATION

School	Name and Address	Circle Highest Year Completed	Type of Degree	Major Subject
HIGH SCHOOL LAST ATTENDED		1 2 3 4		
COLLEGE, UNIVERSITY OR TECHNICAL SCHOOL		1 2 3 4		
COLLEGE, UNIVERSITY OR TECHNICAL SCHOOL		1 2 3 4		
OTHER (Specify)				

List Friends or Relatives Working for This Company

Name_____ Position_____ Dept._____

Name_____ Position_____ Dept._____

PREVIOUS EMPLOYMENT—BEGIN WITH PRESENT OR MOST RECENT POSITION

1. Employer May we contact? Yes_____ No_____	Employed From To
Address (include Street, City, State and Zip code)	Telephone Number
Starting Position	Salary
Last Position	Salary
Name and Title of Last Supervisor	Telephone Number

Brief description of duties:

Reason for Leaving:

Disadvantages of Last Position:

Fig. 7-1 Continued

2. Employer May we contact? Yes_____   No_____ | Employed From To

Address (include Street, City, State and Zip code) | Telephone Number

Starting Position | Salary

Last Position | Salary

Name and Title of Last Supervisor | Telephone Number

Brief description of duties:

Reason for Leaving

Disadvantages of Last Position:

IF MORE THAN TWO PREVIOUS EMPLOYERS, PLEASE LIST OTHERS HERE

Employment Dates From To	Company and Address	Position or Type of Work	Salary or Wage	Reason for Leaving

Please indicate if you were employed under a different name than the one shown on the first page of this application in any of your previous positions.

Employer | Name Used

REFERENCES—OTHER THAN RELATIVES OR FORMER EMPLOYERS

Name | Occupation

Address | Phone Number

Name | Occupation

Address | Phone Number

Employment is dependent upon satisfactorily meeting the medical standards for hire.

Permission is given to investigate previous employment, educational background and references. I release from all liability or responsibility all persons and corporations requesting or supplying information. The facts set forth in my application are true and complete. I understand that false statements on this application shall be considered sufficient cause for rating me ineligible for employment or for dismissal after employment.

Date_____   Signature of Applicant_____

must be relevant and job-related. Certain questions, such as a person's sex, should only be asked if they are job-related. Table 3-2 reviews inappropriate and appropriate questions that are based on federal laws and guidelines. In addition, some states, through their Fair Employment Practice Office, have detailed guidelines on preemployment questions.

On the front of the application form, an equal employment opportunity legend should appear. It may read as follows: "ABC Foodservice Company is an equal employment opportunity employer and does not discriminate based on race, religion, national origin, gender, or handicapped condition in which the person is able to perform the essential functions of the position."

At the end of each application, several statements should appear as follows, and the applicant should sign the application just below them.

- A statement that all information given is true and that the applicant accepts the employer's right to terminate employment if any information is later found to be false should be signed by the applicant.
- A statement should also appear saying that the applicant accepts that there is no promise of permanent employment intended, nor can anyone within the company promise permanent employment without a written contract. This statement stems from the fact that courts have supported employees who were terminated in spite of an implied contract between employer and employee that employment was to continue unless there was a just or reasonable cause. .
- The applicant should also sign a statement allowing prior employers to release information and to release them from any liability for disclosure of such information.

Even if an applicant presents a resume, an application should be filled out. Resumes give the employer only the information the applicant wants the employer to know. Applications ask for information based on the employer's needs.

Once an application has been completed, it should be screened to determine if the applicant might go through any further selection procedures. While reviewing applications, ask yourself the following questions, being very careful not to jump to any conclusions but, rather, to make notes of questions to ask the applicant in order to get more information.

Will the writing meet job requirements for legibility, neatness, spelling, or grammar? Did the applicant have someone else fill out the application and then sign it? (Check for two styles of handwriting.)

Is there any information that was requested but was not provided?

Are there any instructions which were not followed?

How does the applicant's work experience compare with the minimum job requirements? Do previous jobs show preferences for certain types of work?

Do any of the job titles require further explanation?

Does the applicant have a history of changing jobs frequently?

What are the reasons given for changing jobs?

Are there any significant time gaps between jobs?

What is the pattern of the applicant's salary history?

Is there a pattern of increasing job responsibility and pay rates?

How does the applicant's education and training compare to the minimum job requirements?

Preemployment Testing

Preemployment testing covers a wide variety of testing devices which are used to help select the best candidate for the job. Performance tests, knowledge tests, psychological tests, and preemployment physical examinations are examples which will be discussed. Tests such as these do not measure the whole person but, rather, just one or a few dimensions.

All tests must meet guidelines for nondiscrimination according to the EEO Uniform Guidelines on Employee Selection. In other words, tests must be related to successful performance on the job (in other words, be valid) and must yield consistent results (in other words, be reliable). Tests must be given to all applicants, with a single standard for rating scores, and must be given under the same conditions. Even when a test is given to all concerned, it may be considered discriminatory if it eliminates members of protected groups more frequently than members of nonprotected groups.

PERFORMANCE TESTS

Performance tests require candidates to perform part of the job for which they have applied. For example, an applicant for a cooking position may be asked to make a given recipe, or a front-of-the-house employee in a restaurant may be asked to set a table after he or she has seen how they are to be set. An advantage of performance tests is their job-relatedness; however, they are time-consuming, partly because they must be done with applicants on an individual basis. Also, they require an appropriate area in which to do them.

KNOWLEDGE TESTS

Knowledge tests require candidates to complete written test questions. Figure 7-2 shows a written test for cooks. Knowledge tests should test for basic knowledge which is a prerequisite for the job. Like performance tests, knowledge tests are job-related.

PSYCHOLOGICAL TESTS

The following tests that will be discussed are written psychological tests which are available both commercially and custom-made. Each needs to be evaluated in terms of its legality, its cost, the time it takes to administer and score it, and corporate policy concerning it.

Most psychological tests are written tests designed to measure aspects of personality that affect performance. Examples include attitude, honesty, and personality tests. Attitude tests measure attitudes, feelings, and beliefs about concepts, such as supervising or working long hours.

Honesty tests are the most commonly used paper-and-pencil psychological tests. They have become much more popular as an alternative to polygraphs. They are used to locate high-risk applicants for positions in which dishonesty would be damaging to the organization and particularly in which dishonesty would be hard to detect. They often include questions such as the following:

"Should a person be fired if he or she is caught stealing $5?"
"What percentage of people take more than $1 a week from their employer?"
"Do you know if some of your friends steal from their employer?"
"Compared to other people, how honest are you?"

Depending on the answers given, an applicant is rated along a scale that distinguishes between more and less honest individuals.

Honesty tests are relatively inexpensive, objective, not offensive to candidates, and quick to administer; however, there are concerns about their validity. The Reid Honesty Test is a four-part paper-and-

Fig. 7-2 PREEMPLOYEE TEST FOR COOK

COOK'S PREEMPLOYMENT TEST

Directions: Match the cooking method with the correct definition by placing the letter of the definition next to the appropriate number.

Cooking Method	Definition

_____ 1. Boil

_____ 2. Simmer

_____ 3. Poach

_____ 4. Steam

_____ 5. Braise

_____ 6. Roast/bake

_____ 7. Barbecue

_____ 8. Broil

_____ 9. Pan-broil

_____ 10. Grill

_____ 11. Sear

_____ 12. Saute

_____ 13. Deep-fry

_____ 14. Pan-fry

_____ 15. Stir-fry

A. To cook in a hot liquid (at 160–180° F) that is bubbling at the bottom of the pot but is otherwise calm

B. To cook (usually meat) at a high temperature briefly to produce browning, which adds color and flavor to the food

C. To cook uncovered in a saute pan or skillet without adding any fat or liquid; fat is drained off as it accumulates

D. To cook in a boiling liquid (212° F) or to cook the liquid itself at a boil

E. To cook in a liquid that is just below boiling (212° F) and has bubbles floating slowly to the surface

F. To cook food completely covered in hot fat

G. To cook quickly over high heat in a small amount of fat

H. To cook in a small amount of liquid in a covered container at a low heat (300–325° F)

I. To cook uncovered with heated air, usually in an enclosed space

J. To roast using dry heat created by burning wood or hot coals

K. To cook in a pan over moderate heat in a small to moderate amount of fat

L. To cook with direct heat from above

M. To cook small-sized foods over high heat in a small amount of oil

N. To cook with steam, either with or without pressure

O. To cook on an open grate with direct heat from below

Fig. 7-2 Continued

Directions: Fill in the blank space with the correct answer.

16. 1 cup = _____ tablespoon(s)

17. 1 cup = _____ fluid ounce(s)

18. 1 quart = _____ cup(s)

19. 1 tablespoon = _____ teaspoon(s)

20. 1 pound = _____ ounce(s)

21. # means _____

22. lb. means _____

23. oz. means _____

24. Tbsp. means _____

25. tsp. means _____

26–30. Convert the following recipe to yield 150 portions.

Soft Roll Dough

100 portions	150 portions
12 lb. flour	_____ flour
8 lb. water	_____ water
6 oz. yeast	_____ yeast
1½ lb. dry milk	_____ dry milk
12 oz. sugar	_____ sugar

pencil test that can be completed in 45 minutes. It asks questions about personal honesty, drug use, and attitudes toward punishment of theft. Results of honesty tests, as of any tests, should be kept confidential.

The London House Corporation has designed a paper-and-pencil test for hourly employees, referred to as the "Personnel Selection Inventory," which has ten different test forms. It tests for some of the following: honesty, drug avoidance, attitude toward customer relations, emotional stability, safety, employability index, and detailed personal and behavioral history. It costs about $20 to administer and can be completed in less than an hour. Other tests are available which measure "service orientation," which examine an individual's disposition to be helpful, thoughtful, considerate, and cooperative.

When purchasing written tests, you should ask these three questions regarding legality.

1. Does the test have proven validity and reliability based on scientific research? Ask for independently published research studies and the technical manual. Ask exactly what the test has been validated for. The only way to tell if a test accurately predicts future behavior is if it has been given to a group of job applicants whose on-the-job performance was then studied. The individuals studied should also be similar to the type of employees you are testing, with comparable cultural backgrounds, and language and reading skills. Study results should include the percentage of people who were incorrectly predicted to fail, such as the percentage of people who are labeled "dishonest" but are, in fact, honest. A local college professor who teaches statistics could help with this analysis.

2. Does the test comply with Title VII and the EEO Uniform Guidelines on Employee Selection? Although some vendors state that their test is approved by the Equal Employment Opportunity Commission (EEOC), the EEOC does not preapprove tests. Although the EEOC has detailed standards for validating tests, the only time it can be determined if a certain test meets the standards is when someone makes a formal complaint against the test in court.

3. Was the test developed using the Standards for Educational and Psychological Testing of the American Psychological Association?

When you are choosing written tests, also watch out for the following claims made by their vendors (Inwald, 1990).

- "Our test is fully validated." A test can never be fully validated, because validation is a process that does not have a distinct end-point.
- "Our research establishing our test as valid is proprietary in nature." Any company that has done appropriate studies to demonstrate test validity would not hesitate to have them published, since this would be most beneficial to the company.
- "Our test is legal, as stated by our lawyers in this letter." Lawyers lack the expertise to determine if a test has been properly validated.
- "Our test is 85 percent reliable." Sometimes vendors try to get you confused about validity and reliability. Reliability tells us that if someone takes the same test twice, the results will be the same. Reliability is much easier to prove than validity.
- "Our test can be used like an application blank, and you can use the information to start your selection procedures. When used in this manner, validation studies are not needed." Even though tests can be used to gather data, they still need to be validated.

Despite the time and trouble required to choose or develop properly designed written tests, they provide one of our best sources of information for selection decisions. Established written tests have generally been found to be more reliable and valid than the favored evaluation technique, the interview, or other methods which require some amount of human judgment.

Personality tests, such as the Minnesota Multiphasic Inventory, are designed to reveal psychological characteristics that are felt to be relevant to a particular job. Different tests focus on psychological characteristics, such as emotional stability or ability to handle stress. They are more complex, expensive, and time-consuming than honesty tests. They are also more likely to be used in sensitive jobs or upper level jobs, or both.

MEDICAL EXAMINATIONS AND DRUG TESTING

Some employers require medical examinations. State or local agencies may require them for food handlers, and many health care institutions require them for all new employees in the foodservice department, despite their expense. As with all tests, if one applicant must undergo a medical examination, all must. An employee who simply does not appear healthy should not be singled out for an examination, even if the individual does not meet the health requirements.

Drug testing is probably the most controversial preemployment test. Some states have laws regulating their use, and laws are just now being developed in this area, so it is best to obtain the advice of a lawyer.

Background Investigation

The most common form of background investigation is the reference check. According to the Bureau of National Affairs, about 90 percent of employers use a reference check to verify previous employment information, and 50 percent verify education information. Only the application form and interview are more widely used as selection techniques. Checking references has several purposes: to make sure the information is not misstated, to provide additional information on the applicant, and to reduce the possibility of being sued for negligent hiring.

A major concern regarding reference checks has been whether the person used as a reference is willing to provide detailed, candid information about an applicant. This problem stems from the Family Educational Rights Privacy Act of 1974 (FERPA), which gives students the right to examine their school files in order to know whether the file contained any false or damaging information. Eventually, FERPA was extended to include employee personnel records. Because employees can now read reference letters which previously employers were not legally required to reveal, employers are tending to dilute their reference letters after seeing applicants take legal measures, such as suing for slander or defamation of character, because they disagreed with information in the letters. Approximately one-third of all defamation lawsuits are employment-related, and the employee has an excellent chance of winning such a case (Lefever and Abbott).

In a survey of human resource managers, 43 percent judged the reference letter to be somewhat valuable, and 38 percent judged it to be of little value (Von der Embse and Wyse, 1985). To increase the usefulness of reference letters, employers can do three things. First, they can have the applicant fill out and sign forms to be used in checking references, and ask applicants if they wish to sign a statement waiving their rights to see the completed reference letters. Second, they can ask the applicant to sign a statement (typically, on the application—see Fig. 7-1) allowing prior employers to release information and also release them from any liability for disclosure of such information. Third, employers can be as specific as possible about the information they would like in order to increase the possibility of getting reliable, thorough information.

Most managers prefer checking references by phone, since this method gives more useful, candid information and is relatively inexpensive and fast. Be sure to document your phone calls on a reference form, which can be used for both verbal and written references (Fig. 7-3). It is best to start your reference check with the Human Resources or Personnel Department to verify information such as job titles, dates of employment, and salary history. Always identify yourself, your company, and explain that you are doing a reference check.

Next, ask to speak to the applicant's former supervisor. Identify yourself again and tell this person that the information is confidential. Start out by confirming objective information, such as job titles, attendance record, and so on. Once you feel the former employer will volunteer more information, you can switch from "yes-no" type questions to those asking for more information. But do not be surprised if this person informs you that he or she will not supply you with any other information than the Human Resources Department just gave you. Be confident, persistent, and assertive; however, if you get nowhere, it is not unusual.

Guidelines for Checking References

- It is more beneficial for the person doing the interview to check the references.
- Always check references of two or more past employers to get a more complete and accurate assessment.
- If you check references on one applicant, do so on all applicants. Never single out an applicant for reference checks. Consistency here is important to avoid charges of discrimination.
- If an applicant is rejected because of a negative job reference, make sure the concern is job-related. Then, document it and allow the applicant to respond to it. Do not forget that most applicants have probably encountered on-the-job problems at least once, perhaps due to a mismatch of personalities or many other reasons. Also, do not forget that former employers who lost a good employee may be bitter, and employers who dismissed an employee frequently offer to give the employee a neutral job reference to help the employee out the door.
- If you really need to get a reference from the applicant's current job for whatever the reason, you can, if it is a management position, ask to speak with his or her peers. Another solution is to offer the applicant the job, provided he or she is the best choice, and

Fig. 7-3 SAMPLE TELEPHONE REFERENCE CHECK FORM

TELEPHONE REFERENCE CHECK

Applicant Name: _____

Position Applied for: _____

Name of Company, Location, and Phone Number: _____

_____

_____

_____

Name and Title of Person Supplying Reference: _____

_____

1. What are the dates of employment when he or she was employed by you? _____

2. What was his or her title when he or she started working for you, and when he or she left the company? _____

_____

3. What was the starting and ending salary? _____

_____

4. What were his or her primary job duties and responsibilities? _____

_____

_____

_____

5. How much supervision did he or she receive? _____

_____

6. How were his or her attendance and lateness records? _____

_____

7. What was this person's reason for leaving? _____

_____

8. Did he or she do a satisfactory job? _____

_____

9. In what areas were job skills excellent? In what areas were job skills weak?_____

_____

Fig. 7-3 Continued

10. Did this individual get along well with others? _____

    _____

    _____

11. Would you rehire this individual? Why or why not? _____

    _____

    _____

_____   _____

Date   Name

make it contingent upon getting a good reference from the current employer once the applicant has resigned. For a management position, it is not a bad idea to ask each applicant for names of a superior, a peer, and a subordinate with whom he or she has worked in the past 3 to 5 years.

When you are checking an applicant's educational background, you can contact companies that offer verification services, such as the National Credential Verification Service in Minneapolis. They can also verify professional memberships and awards. The major use of checking educational references is to confirm that the information given is true. Falsifying academic degrees is not unusual. Most often you will need to verify the possession of degrees and certifications. If you want a transcript of an applicant's work, you will need written permission from the applicant to obtain the transcript.

Another way of checking an employee's background is through the use of public records. Employers can look at criminal records, driving records, workers' compensation records, and federal court records. Information from these sources can be used to disqualify an applicant only if the information is job-related and such information is consistently applied in the selection process.

Criminal records are available either through a state central repository or the county. Obtaining records through the county tends to be quicker and less costly, and it often will give information on the phone. Information obtained from the county is usually more complete than that obtained from the state, but if many counties have to be contacted, it may be easier for you to just contact the state.

Driving records are available through a state motor vehicle office. Generally, driving records can be obtained by mail and are inexpensive. An employer can use this information to cross-check date of birth, and so on, to see if the information has been falsified.

Workers' compensation records can reveal whether or not a candidate has a past history of injuring himself or herself on the job and, if so, whether the candidate has been cleared to resume full duties. These records are available through the state.

Unless business necessity can be proved, it is not appropriate to use an applicant's financial status when you are making an employment decision. There is no evidence that applicants with credit problems will be poor employees or will be more likely to steal. In addition, it is probable that this practice would discriminate against some minority groups.

A final reference source is personal references, if they have been requested on the application. In general, they offer little productive information, but they may have to be contacted if other reference sources do not exist, as when teenagers are looking for their first job. You may get more insight into an applicant by seeing exactly whom they listed as personal references.

Errors in Evaluation

A major error related to evaluating applicants results when the evaluator is subjective about the individual, rather than objective. Each person who evaluates applicants brings to the rating process personal attitudes, values, perceptions, prejudices, stereotypes, and emotions. Personal values and prejudices, for example, can actually cause an evaluator to keep from focusing on the job requirements.

Related to the problem of remaining objective is that of stereotyping applicants. A common stereotype in foodservice is that chefs are always temperamental. A more universal stereotype is that female employees with children will take more time off than male employees.

The "halo effect" refers to letting the rating of one factor in which an employee does very well, such as being very friendly and easygoing, positively influence the rating of other factors. The opposite of the "halo effect" is the "horns effect," in which a poor rating in one aspect of the evaluation negatively influences the rating of other factors.

Evaluators may make errors if they rate an applicant solely on their own first impressions. For instance, if an applicant comes in for an interview with an unkempt appearance, the interviewer may decide that this individual cannot possibly be a good choice. An evaluator may also assume incorrectly that an applicant is an excellent choice because he or she is good-looking, tall, or young. Employees do not have to be tall, attractive, and young to do a good job.

Another common error is to evaluate highly an applicant who is just like the evaluator, whether the applicant deserves the high evaluation or not. Organizations typically function better when there is diversity of personalities and experiences.

When evaluating applicants, it is best that you screen out subjective thoughts and not jump to any conclusions. Concentrate on getting the full picture and on keeping an open mind.

8

Interviewing

After applications, the most frequently used method for judging and selecting applicants is the interview. Almost all, if not all, jobs are filled by applicants who go through an interview, despite the fact that interviews are very time-consuming and are not usually as accurate as other methods, such as preemployment testing and biographical data (once verified). Interviewing is a complex process requiring the interviewer to maintain a smooth social exchange while simultaneously gathering and processing information. This can be difficult for an individual who lacks appropriate training and experience. This chapter will cover the basics of interviewing.

Purposes

Why should applicants be interviewed, especially when an interview takes so much time? Is interviewing worth the time involved? If it is done properly, interviewing can serve many purposes, such as getting information on which to base a decision; observing personal characteristics, motivations, and goals; informing the applicant more fully about the job and the company; and establishing the basis for a possible future working relationship.

A good interviewer uses the interview to examine what is referred to as "can-do" and "will-do" factors. Can-do factors are covered in the job requirements: the knowledge, skills and abilities, work experience and training, and education. Will-do factors include motivation, work interests, and personal characteristics. Some applicants can do the job without any problem; however, they may lack the motivation or interest required to do the job well. Therefore, an interview can be used to judge whether or not the applicant can do the job well, as well as whether or not the applicant will do the job.

Interviewing Errors

Interviewing is a skill that requires practice, yet practice does not always make perfect. Mistakes are often made when the questions asked do little to elicit information from the applicant. The list that follows provides examples of each type of interview questions discussed here.

OPEN-ENDED

What in your background qualifies you for this position?

Can you tell me something about the boss you most liked working for?

How did you feel about working with customers?

CLOSED-ENDED

Do you like your present job?

How long were you in your last job?

REFLECTIVE

Do you mean you left your last job because they did not pay you enough?

Am I hearing you tell me that you have good interpersonal relation skills?

PROBING

What are some of the reasons you left your last job?

What has been your experience in serving guests?

SITUATIONAL

In your current job, what do you usually do when a customer complains about the food?

If your boss asked you to do something that you disagreed with, such as discipline someone, what would you do?

LEADING
Wouldn't you prefer the night shift?
We are looking for a motivated person for this position. Are you
   motivated?

LOADED
Are you saying you are pro-union or anti-union?

Closed-ended interview questions can be answered with a "yes" or
"no" or a specific piece of information. Almost any closed-ended or
direct question could be asked in an open-ended manner. Open-ended
questions require the applicant to discuss something about himself
or herself. They are useful for getting much information and allow for
observation of verbal communication skills, but they should not be
too broad in scope. They also provide clues for further questions.
Reflective questions restate what the applicant has said in an at-
tempt to gain clarification. Probing questions ask for more information. Examples include questions about why or how something hap-
pened. Situational questions ask what the applicant would do in given
situations. These situations may be hypothetical, but it has been found
that if real situations are used, more realistic feedback is obtained.
Two types of questions to avoid are leading questions and loaded
questions. Leading questions give the desired answer to the applicant.
Loaded questions force an applicant to choose between two choices,
both choices being undesirable.
Depending on the type of information desired, different types of
questions are appropriate. To learn the most about an applicant,
open-ended, reflective, probing, and situational questions should be
asked. Closed-ended questions should be used sparingly.
Following are other errors which an interviewer may make.

- The interviewer does too much talking. The applicant should be
  doing most of the talking (about 80 percent), and the interviewer
  should be actively listening.
- The interviewer predicts the applicant's ability to do the job based
  on a first impression, such as an impression or assumption about
  an applicant's clothing, hairstyle, or jewelry. This same type of
  error may occur during the interview when the interviewer jumps
  to conclusions based on a single statement made by the applicant.
  No assumptions should be made until all information is in.
- The interviewer makes subjective evaluations. Each interviewer
  brings to the interview situation personal values, perceptions,
  prejudices, stereotypes, and emotions, and may use them to judge

or to evaluate others. It is crucial that the interviewer remain objective.

- Research has shown that factors such as verbal fluency, age, sex, and attractiveness of an applicant can influence the outcome of an interview.
- Sometimes body language is misread by an interviewer. This happens most often when the interviewer interprets body language according to his or her own gestures or expressions.
- Interviewers also make the "similar-to-me" mistake by favoring an applicant who is just like him or her in terms of background, preferences, or appearance.
- The interviewer leads the interview in a totally unstructured or highly structured fashion. When the interviewer gives little or no structure to the interview, a friendly chat (which achieves little) typically ensues. On the other hand, when the interviewer overly structures the interview by following a list of questions, it limits the discussion and the applicant does not usually open up.
- The interviewer does not get the applicant to open up.
- The interviewer puts the applicant under stress. This usually hinders the interviewer from learning about the applicant's actual abilities.
- The interviewer makes judgments about an applicant based on a comparison with the previous applicant. For instance, an applicant with average credentials may be ranked very highly if he or she is interviewed after someone who was ranked very low.

The Interview Process

An interview requires much more than simply meeting the applicant on time and interviewing him or her for an appropriate period of time. You need time before the interview to prepare your questions and also time after the interview to focus your thoughts on how well the applicant meets job requirements.

How much time an interview should take will vary depending on the nature of the job. An hourly, or nonexempt, position may require from 30 to 45 minutes for the interview itself. Interviewing for supervisory or managerial level positions generally requires more time, from 45 to 90 minutes. In addition to the interview time, another 15 to 30 minutes are needed to get certain tasks done before and after the interview.

There are differing philosophies on how to conduct an interview. Some interviewers prefer to go through a set of questions with the candidate. Others prefer to ask questions in a more off-the-cuff, unstructured fashion. Both styles have their advantages and disadvantages. By using a set of predetermined questions related to the job requirements, managers are sure not to forget anything, and it will be easier for them to compare applicants. They are also being consistent among all candidates but may fail to dig into areas revealed during the interview. On the other hand, when managers question applicants in a more relaxed manner, they are able to put more concentration on areas as the need arises, but unfortunately these interviews are much more susceptible to gathering little information and making premature decisions about a candidate. It also increases the chances of forgetting to get a crucial piece of information and of asking a question that is not related to the job.

Therefore, the best approach is to integrate both philosophies; in other words, interviewers should have predetermined questions that they would like to ask, but they do not need to follow them religiously. Questions can be divided into the four areas of job qualifications: knowledge, skills and abilities, work experience, and education and training. Use your set of questions as a starting point or guide with which to elicit feedback from the applicant.

BEFORE THE INTERVIEW

Before the interview, there is preparation work which needs to be done.

- Review the application, and resume when applicable, once again in order to jot down any additional questions.
- Be sure to review the job description and have a copy available to the applicant.
- It is a good idea to make a written record of your interview. Figure 8-1 is an interviewer's evaluation form which can be used to help evaluate applicants as well as to document information obtained during the interview. The job qualifications from the job description should be inserted in the appropriate column prior to the interview.
- Collect any brochures, and so on, that you would like to give the applicant which describe the company and its internal organization, benefits, and so forth.

Fig. 8-1 FORM FOR INTERVIEWER TO EVALUATE APPLICANT

INTERVIEWER'S EVALUATION FORM

Date: _____

Applicant's Name: _____

Position/Department: _____

Job Qualifications	Applicant's Qualifications	Does Not Meet Qualification	Meets Minimum Qualification	Exceeds Qualification
1. Knowledge				
2. Skills and Abilities				
3. Work Experience				
4. Education and Training				

Fig. 8-1   Continued

Applicant's Salary Requirements: _____

Can applicant work the schedule or hours required? _____

Level of interest in job: Low   Moderate   High

Overall evaluation: _____ Fails to meet some or all job qualifications

_____ Meets all job qualifications

_____ Exceeds job qualifications

Additional Comments:

_____

_____

_____

_____

Interviewer's Signature

- Arrange for a quiet place for the interview which will be private and without distractions or interruptions.
- Anyone else who will be involved in the interview process should be alerted.

STARTING THE INTERVIEW

Always start the interview on time, greet the applicant warmly by name, and introduce yourself by name and title. This is a crucial time in which to develop rapport with the applicant. A seating arrangement that does not put a desk or a table between you and the applicant is also conducive to developing rapport; however, if you are more comfortable behind a desk, sit there. Start with some small talk on a neutral topic or offer the applicant a cup of coffee as a way to create an informal, relaxed atmosphere and to develop rapport. Some popular ice-breakers are as follows:

Did you have any trouble getting here?
Did you have any trouble parking?
Isn't it a lovely day!
I noticed you went to college in Vermont. How did you like it there?

Do not spend more than a couple of minutes warming up.
At this point, let us discuss an outline of the interview process.

THE ACTUAL INTERVIEW

Following are the primary areas to be discussed during the heart of the interview. They are often discussed in this order, and each area should be completely covered before you proceed to the next.

1. Gather and analyze information about the applicant's knowledge, skills and abilities, work experience, and education and training.
2. Explain the job fully, including duties, hours of work, overtime requirements, policies and procedures, wages and benefits, probationary period, performance reviews, training, incentive programs, and growth opportunities. Inform the applicant that he or she will have to provide proof of being able to work in the United States, as well as proof of age, if it is required for the job.

Make clear all expectations, including performance standards, if they are applicable. Give the applicant the job description.
3. Explain the company's goals, history, and structure. Sell the applicant on your company and what it has to offer, being of course honest and realistic. Give the applicant any company information.
4. Ask the applicant whether he or she has anything to add or any questions to ask.

Some interviewers prefer to start the interview by briefly describing the company or the job opening. In this manner, the applicant will feel more at ease. It is important not to give too much information at this time as the applicant may later parrot back all the supposedly correct responses. Others prefer to ask "Would you tell me what you do during a typical day on the job?" This question allows the applicant to discuss a familiar subject and gives the interviewer a chance to evaluate verbal skills and to get information in order to ask further questions.

Tips for Interviewing

▪ Use open-ended, reflective, probing, and situational questions.
▪ Be nonjudgmental during the entire interview process. Do not jump to conclusions. A poor interviewer reaches a decision in the first five minutes.
▪ Recognize your own personal biases and try not to let them influence you. Screen out any ethnocentric thoughts. Be objective. Do not look for clones of yourself. Do not let an applicant's age, sex, attractiveness, or verbal fluency influence your opinions.
▪ Spend most of your time listening attentively. Allow the candidate to do at least 70 to 80 percent of the talking, and restrict your talking to 20 to 30 percent at most. Listen to each answer before deciding on the next question. Do not interrupt!
▪ Make notes openly on the Interviewer's Evaluation Form (Fig. 8-1) so that vital information is not forgotten. Record key points. Explain to the applicant at the beginning of the interview that you will be taking notes to help get information recorded. Most applicants will not mind this, since they want you to remember as much about them as possible.
▪ Repeat or paraphrase the applicant's statements to ascertain a better understanding and to get more information, such as "So you were responsible for the dining room staff in that job. . . ." Or repeat the last few words the applicant just said with a ques-

tioning inflection. Also, periodically summarize the applicant's statements to clarify points and to bring information together. A summary statement may begin with, "Let's state the major points up to now. . . ." In this manner, the applicant can confirm or clarify what has been discussed. Paraphrasing and summarizing are also good techniques to use to get an applicant to talk and show interest.

- Another technique to get a quiet applicant to talk and show interest is to use pauses to allow the applicant to sense that more information is desired and hopefully feel more compelled to talk. During this time, you can observe the applicant's poise. Also, use certain phrases such as "I see," "How interesting," and "I didn't know that" to encourage the applicant to talk. Any phrases used should indicate interest, not agreement or disagreement. Avoid agreeing or disagreeing.

- Use body language to show interest and elicit information. Use direct eye contact, nod, smile, and lean slightly forward.

- Do not be bashful about probing for more information when it is called for, such as when an applicant talks very briefly or vaguely about an important topic. Usually, applicants do not want to discuss a bad experience they may have had. If unfavorable information is revealed, make a comment like "That happens to all of us at one time or another" to defuse the situation. You should wait until the latter part of the interview to discuss any concerns you may have about the applicant.

- Instead of asking about an applicant's "weaknesses," refer to "areas of improvement."

- Paint a realistic picture of the job. Be honest. Make no promises you cannot keep and provide information freely. Young people who are looking for their first job often have unrealistic expectations and need to know about a job's drawbacks, such as night and weekend hours. Painting a realistic job picture reduces employee dissatisfaction and turnover.

- Speak in language which the applicant will understand.

- Always be sincere, respectful, courteous, friendly, and treat all applicants in the same way.

CLOSING THE INTERVIEW

In closing the interview, you should allow time for the applicant to ask any further questions. At the same time, the applicant should be asked about his or her interest in the job and should be told when a hiring decision will be made and how he or she will be notified. In some cases, the interview may be followed by some type of testing or a second interview, which should then be discussed, along with a time frame. Always close on a positive note and thank the applicant for his or her time.

AFTER THE INTERVIEW

Instead of rushing off to another concern, take the time to think things over, while they are still clear, and finish writing up the Interviewer's Evaluation Form. When you are writing about an interview, avoid writing down any subjective, opinionated observations, such as "The candidate was pretentious . . . rude . . . curt . . . boring . . . sarcastic." Instead, write down job-related facts and direct observations, not inferences or impressions. Strive to be objective, factual, and clear as in the following statements.

Applicant appears well-groomed and neatly dressed.
Applicant has not worked in a foodservice operation but "I work with food at home every day."
Applicant states she wants to work "for the money."
Applicant smiled throughout most of 30-minute interview.

This is also a good time for you to check references and set up any additional appointments.

9

Selecting and Hiring

After you have used various techniques, such as interviews, to evaluate applicants, it is time to make the selection, hire the individual, and orient the new hire. This chapter will discuss each of these topics.

Selection

Selection is the process by which a company chooses from a list of applicants the person (or persons) who best meets the qualifications of the position available. The purpose of making the selection is to pick the person most likely to meet the performance standards. This is not usually a simple task. The selection of applicants must be based on the person's knowledge, skills and abilities, work experience, and education and training as they relate to the job qualifications. Any criteria used in the selection process must be consistently and directly related to job performance.

By using the Comparison of Applicants for Selection Form (Fig. 9-1), you can compare the various applicants. Selection can be complicated, because the best candidate if you have used one method, such as preemployment testing, may not be the best candidate if you have used another method, such as interviewing. This form helps to give you the total picture.

Fig. 9-1 FORM TO COMPARE APPLICANTS FOR SELECTION

COMPARISON OF APPLICANTS FOR SELECTION

Date: _____

Position/Department to be filled: _____

First, fill in the job qualifications for this position. Next, rate each applicant using this scale:

1 Does not meet qualification
2 Meets minimum qualification
3 Exceeds qualification

Job Qualifications	Applicant	Applicant	Applicant	Applicant
1. Knowledge				
2. Skills and Abilities				
3. Work Experience				
4. Education and Training				

Fig. 9-1 Continued

Rate each applicant using this scale.

   1   Unsatisfactory results

   2   Satisfactory results

   3   Above average results

	Applicant	Applicant	Applicant	Applicant
Preemployment Testing				
Test 1				
Test 2				
Test 3				
Test 4				
Background Checks				
Reference 1				
Reference 2				
Reference 3				
Reference 4				
Reference 5				
Totals				

Final Selection: _____

Name of Person(s) Making Selection: _____

Tips for Making the Selection Decision

- Be prepared to spend some time making the selection decision. This decision should not be done hastily as the average cost of hiring an unskilled hourly employee is between $400 and $1,500, or typically up to one month's pay. These figures can go up to $2,000 to $3,000 for skilled employees such as line cooks and servers. This basically covers the expenses for recruiting and selecting a new candidate, doing all the necessary paperwork for the new employee such as payroll and benefit records, training the worker, and covering overtime costs incurred while the position is vacant, as well as any severance pay. And worse than the dollar cost incurred is how poor selection practices tend to lower both employee morale and quality of service as well as cause stress for managers.

- Every job requires that workers function in some degree in relation to people, data, and things. Be sure to select applicants who enjoy being with people for jobs involving direct customer contact. Applicants who prefer to work with data such as numbers may prefer to do purchasing or accounting work. Applicants who like to work with things such as food may prefer taking care of storage areas or cooking.

- When the best candidate for a job is overqualified, there is often concern that this individual will leave the job after a better opportunity comes up or be bored and unproductive until this happens. This is not always the case, depending on the candidate's motivation for taking the job and whether this candidate may be moved into a higher position fairly quickly. Each situation should be looked at individually.

Hiring

The hiring process begins by offering the job to the applicant selected and continues through the period during which this individual is oriented to his or her new job.

MAKING AND CLOSING THE OFFER

Offers for all jobs should be made in writing. The offer letter typically is sent to, or given to, the new hire after an offer has been made and accepted over the phone. When you are making an offer, be sure to include all conditions discussed with the applicant, such as relocation assistance or immediate health coverage. When the applicant has to remind you of any conditions, it makes you and your company look bad. Negotiating any employment conditions should be done in a professional manner and should be worked out before an offer is made. Figure 9-2 shows a sample offer letter which is positive and complimentary. The following points should appear in this letter, some of which are appropriate under certain circumstances:

Position title
Supervisor
Department
Location
Salary
Schedule or shift, days off
When job starts (date and time), where to report, whom to report
　to, and when job ends on the first day
Clothing and equipment needed
Meal arrangements
Parking
Arrangements for orientation
Someone's name and phone number for applicant to contact with
　questions
Description of benefits program available
Appointment time or whom to call for an appointment concerning
　filling out of personnel forms (such as the I-9 form)
Employment contract
Probationary period
Relocation assistance
Any other conditions of employment

At the bottom of the letter there should appear a statement which the new hire should sign, stating that he or she agrees with the hiring conditions. A date should also be mentioned for the signed letter to be returned.

Employment contracts are typically reserved for managers. They usually spell out employment conditions, including when an employer could terminate the manager. The purpose of these contracts is to avert lawsuits, particularly those concerning wrongful discharge. A labor attorney should always be used to develop any type of employment contract so that it will be legal and will hold up in court.

In terms of making offers, it is important that there be a limited number of people within any company who have the authority to

Fig. 9-2 SAMPLE OFFER LETTER

January 5, 1990

Mr. John Q. Public
15 Main Street
Newtown, Pennsylvania 18960

Dear Mr. Public,

We are pleased to confirm the verbal offer extended this morning for you to join our fine staff as a Dining Room Supervisor. As discussed, you will begin work on Monday, February 1st. On that date, please report to me in my office at 10:00 A.M. I will review your benefits with you and other details at that time. At 11:00 A.M., you will start orientation with your supervisor.

Following are the specific details of your employment.

1. Your title will be Dining Room Supervisor and you will be reporting to Mr. Joe White, Dining Room Manager.
2. Your hours will be 11:00 A.M. to 8:00 P.M., with Mondays off.
3. Your salary will be $24,000 annually. You are entitled to our full benefits package of medical and life insurance, paid days off, and a profit-sharing plan, which will be effective on your first date of employment. Enclosed is a benefits brochure describing the details.
4. The dress code for your position requires a jacket and tie.
5. Staff meals are available to you at no cost.
6. The probationary period for this position is 90 days. At that time you will be evaluated by your supervisor. At any time during this period, either party may terminate the relationship without cause or reason.

Once again, we welcome you to our team and look forward to working with you. Please sign below to show you have reviewed and accept these terms of employment, and return the letter to me no later than January 20th. If you have any questions or concerns, please feel free to contact me at (516)781-8000, extension 107.

Sincerely,

Jack Clark
Personnel Director

JC/ke
enc.

I agree with the hiring conditions stated above.

_____   _____
Signature   Date

make job offers. In this manner, offers are likely to be made in a more consistent manner and there is more control over the process. Unfortunately, employers are taken to court by employees over misunderstandings stemming from the initial offer.

Unfortunately for the employer, once a new hire tells the current employer about the new job, this employer may make a counteroffer which is good enough to convince the new hire not to leave. This is more often the case for salaried employees than hourly employees. It is best to acknowledge to the new hire this possibility and to discuss it openly. Explain that, while counteroffers are not unusual, any promises made are not always kept. Other things you can do when closing the offer to help prevent counteroffers follow.

- Explain that everyone is very pleased that the new hire will be coming on board. Tell him or her that they have made an excellent choice.
- Explain that an announcement will be coming out to notify other staff members.
- Get the new hire's name for a name tag and possibly for business cards.
- Get the new hire's uniform size (if needed).
- For a salaried position, ask the new hire if he or she would like to come in for a few hours before the start date to see more of the operation.

REJECTION LETTERS

Once your new hire accepts the job offer (preferably in writing), you need to write a rejection letter to those applicants who did not get the position. Figure 9-3 contains a sample letter. You should explain to any rejected individuals that you will keep their applications on file for consideration for another position in the future. Rejection letters should be brief, sincere, and as positive as possible.

ANNOUNCEMENT OF NEW HIRE

Before a new employee starts working, fellow workers should be informed of the person's name, position, starting date, and possibly past work experience. In the case of managerial employees, it is common practice for written notices to be sent out to appropriate personnel. In the case of hourly employees, they are often informed verbally

Fig. 9-3 SAMPLE REJECTION LETTER

January 5, 1990

Mr. Jay Reynolds
25 Park Street
Holland, Pennsylvania 19067

Dear Mr. Reynolds,

   Thank you for coming in and meeting with us regarding the position of Dining Room Manager. We found your experience and skills to be impressive. However, after examining all factors, we have selected another candidate whose qualifications better match our requirements. Your resume will be kept on file for 6 months in the event another position for which you are qualified becomes available.

   Again, thank you for your time, and we wish you the best of luck in your future endeavors.

Sincerely,

Jack Clark
Personnel Director

JC/ke

at a meeting at which they are asked to welcome the new h... be as helpful as possible.

There is nothing worse to a new hire than showing up at work the first day and being told by the supervisor, "I didn't know you were coming." Likewise, the supervisor is put on the spot, and other employees are all asking each other who this new person is. Doing such a simple thing as announcing the arrival of a new hire can help everyone adjust to the change much more quickly.

PROCESSING OF PERSONNEL RECORDS

Once someone has been hired, processing of the new hire starts. The personnel file should include the following as appropriate to the company, the job, and the employee:

- Staffing requisition
- Application
- Any testing or evaluation results
- Background checks
- Signed offer letter
- Employment contract
- Proof of age
- Work permit
- Social Security number
- Tax withholding forms
- Employment Eligibility Verification (I-9) form
- Bonding application
- Data for EEOC report (see Chapter 3)
- Signed benefit forms

The employee must be present to fill out and sign tax withholding forms, the Employment Eligibility Verification (I-9) form, data for the EEOC report, and benefit forms. There may also be additional paperwork. A new hire may be asked to come in before starting the new job for processing to speed up the process. At the same time, the new hire may be fitted for a uniform, given a preemployment physical, or paperwork filled out for a name tag.

Orientation

When any new employee comes on board, orientation to the job and to the company is needed. Job orientation includes being instructed on how to become proficient at the new job. Company orientation refers to the employee learning about the company and how his or her job fits in with, and contributes to, the company's goals. It could therefore be said that job orientation tells the employee both what the job is and how to do it, and that company orientation tells the employee why.

Unfortunately, orientation for new employees at all levels is overlooked in many foodservices. Very often it is left to chance or to another employee who really has little desire or ability to train new employees. Orientation requires a time commitment, which is tough to find in a business in which there is so much time pressure.

So, if a new hire does not go through an orientation, what happens? Managers will lose control over some very important aspects of their business, such as work methods, quality control, quality service, and performance standards. In other words, the cooks might each provide different size portions for the same menu items, and the guests might not be welcomed quickly or treated very well. Likewise, the costs of not performing orientation are great. Research increasingly indicates that no orientation or poor orientation contributes to new hires' dissatisfaction and turnover (Zemke, 1989).

JOB ORIENTATION

Every day, new employees start their first day on the job with little direction other than where the rest rooms are. Whereas foodservice managers are very concerned about the guest's first impression, they need to be equally concerned about the employee's first impression of the company. Both have a long-lasting effect.

The following is an example of an orientation checklist. It shows the wide range of topics which need to be discussed, as appropriate to the particular operation, during the first days on the job.

INTRODUCTION TO THE COMPANY
_____ Welcome the new employee.
_____ Describe the company briefly, including history, operation (type of menu, service, hours of operation, etc.), and goals. (Be sure to mention the importance of quality service.)
_____ Show how the company is structured or organized.

POLICIES AND PROCEDURES
_____ Explain the dress code and who furnishes uniforms.
_____ Describe where to park.

_____ Explain how to sign in and out and when to do so.

_____ Assign a locker and explain its use.

_____ Review the amount of sick time, holiday time, personal time, and vacation time allowed as applicable.

_____ Explain how the employee is to call in if he or she is unable to come to work.

_____ Explain the procedure for requesting time off.

_____ Review the new employee's salary and when and where to pick up the paycheck, as well as who can pick up the employee's paycheck. If applicable, explain the policy on overtime and reporting of tips.

_____ Discuss the rules on personal telephone use.

_____ Explain the company's smoking policy.

_____ Explain the company's meal policy, including when and where food can be eaten.

_____ Explain channels of communication—meetings, bulletin boards, etc.

_____ Review disciplinary guidelines.

_____ Explain the guest relations policy.

_____ Review the teamwork policy.

_____ Explain the property removal policy.

_____ Explain responsible service of alcohol, if applicable.

_____ Explain the Equal Employment Opportunity policy.

_____ Discuss promotional and transfer opportunities.

_____ Explain the professional conduct policy.

_____ Explain guidelines for safe food handling, safety in the kitchen, and what to do in case of a fire.

_____ Explain requirements for giving notice if employee decides to leave the job.

THE NEW JOB

_____ Review the job description and standards of performance.

_____ Review the daily work schedule, including break times.

_____ Review the hours of work and days off. Show where the schedule is posted.

_____ Explain how and when the employee will be evaluated.

_____ Explain the probationary period.

_____ Explain the training program, including its length.

_____ Describe growth opportunities.

_____ Give a tour of the company's operation and introduce the employee to other managers and coworkers.

The benefit of using such a checklist is that it ensures consistency among managers who are conducting orientation. It also gives the employee the message that orientation is important enough for the company to go about it in an organized and professional manner.

Because the employee is likely to forget much of what is said at this time, all information covered should be given to him or her in a written format. This is often done by developing and handing out to new hires an employee handbook. Employees should sign, either on the orientation checklist or on a page in the employee handbook, that they have been given this information. This then provides documentation that the employee was oriented to the new job.

Initially, the supervisor will be the key person to orient and influence the new employee's first impressions of the company and the job. It is important to give this person the training and support needed to perform these functions.

Probably the most common teaching method used for training new employees is what is commonly referred to as on-the-job training (OJT). With this method, the new employee works with a peer, manager, or supervisor on the actual job. OJT is of little use if the employee is put with someone who either cannot or does not want to train a new person or if the structure of the training is loose. Although this method has been badly abused in what has been called the "buddy system," it has the potential for providing good hands-on experience. What happens is that the job takes priority, so the trainee may not get much explanation of what to do and also may spend too much time doing menial jobs without any significance, such as running for supplies.

OJT can work well when certain conditions are met.

- The trainer must be willing and able to train a new employee.
- The training should be structured with specific duties and tasks to be accomplished within certain time frames.
- The trainer should determine the trainee's past experience.
- Duties, along with their rationale and performance standards, should be taught, and the trainee should be allowed to do parts of the trainer's job, when ready.
- The trainee should be frequently questioned for understanding and trained off the job, as well as on the job, for the best results.

Figures 9-4 to 9-8 show sample OJT checklists.

Selecting a trainer and training that person to do a good job may be difficult. Ideally, a manager or a supervisor is the best choice for training. In the case of on-the-job training, if a competent employee

Fig. 9-4   SAMPLE ON-THE-JOB TRAINING CHECKLIST FOR A SERVER

OJT CHECKLIST—SERVER

Name of Trainee: _____

Date Starting Training: _____

Trainer(s): _____

Write the date in the blank space next to each task when you feel the trainee has mastered it.

General Considerations
_____ Appearance
_____ Conduct at work
_____ Hospitality and courtesy toward guests
_____ Attendance/punctuality
_____ Other _____

Opening Duties and Side Work
_____ Station and table numbers
_____ Folds napkins
_____ Places tablecloths on tables
_____ Sets tables
_____ Stocks stations
_____ Cleans and marries condiments
_____ Refills salt and pepper shakers
_____ Refills sugar bowls
_____ Other _____

Service
_____ The overall sequence of service
_____ Pours water at the table
_____ Numbers the guests at the table
_____ Greets guests and takes the cocktail order
_____ Fills the cocktail order at the service bar
_____ Serves cocktails
_____ Takes the order for appetizers and the main course

Fig. 9-4   **Continued**

_____ Suggests wine

_____ Orders and picks up appetizers

_____ Serves appetizers

_____ Clears and resets the table after appetizers

_____ Serves bread and butter

_____ Orders and picks up wine

_____ Serves wine

_____ Orders and picks up the main course

_____ Serves the main course

_____ Clears and crumbs the table after the main course

_____ Suggests dessert, coffee, and after-dinner drinks

_____ Serves desserts

_____ Serves coffee, tea, and after-dinner drinks

_____ Presents the check and does closing service

Clearing and Resetting the Table

_____ Stacks items on a bus tray

_____ Carries a bus tray

_____ Empties a bus tray by the dish machine

_____ Clears the table and changes the tablecloth after guests have left

_____ Resets tables for the next seating

Handling Guest Checks

_____ Obtains guest checks at the start of service

_____ Knows register keyboard and commands

_____ Knows how to open a check

_____ Enters items on the guest check

_____ Tallies the check at the end of service

_____ Pays the guest check

Product Knowledge

_____ Menu—description and taste of every item on the menu

_____ Wine—background information, description, and taste of wines
on the wine list, recommending wines with food

Fig. 9-4 Continued

_____ Cocktails/liquor—brands stocked, preparation, service, and taste of popular cocktails and speciality drinks

_____ Policies on responsible service of alcohol

Suggestive Selling

_____ Suggestive selling techniques

_____ Sales per guest of $_____ meet or exceed restaurant average of $_____

Closing Duties and Side Work

_____ Washes service trays

_____ Cleans wine buckets

_____ Cleans side stations

_____ Other _____

Please sign below upon completion of training. Both the employee and the trainer certify by their signatures that the training has been adequate to prepare the new employee to function in his or her new position.

_____   _____

Signature/Date (Employee)   Signature/Date (Trainer)

Courtesy of Hospitality Industry Training, Inc., Golden, Colorado.

Fig. 9-5 SAMPLE ON-THE-JOB TRAINING CHECKLIST FOR A HOST/HOSTESS

OJT CHECKLIST—HOST/HOSTESS

Name of Trainee: _____

Date Starting Training: _____

Trainer(s): _____

Write the date in the blank space next to each task when you feel the trainee has mastered it.

Dining Room Operation

_____ Supervises opening duties and sidework

_____ Supervises service and cash handling

_____ Supervises closing duties and sidework

_____ Answers guest questions on menu, wine, cocktails, and liquor served

_____ Takes reservations

_____ Conducts daily meeting with staff

_____ Greets guests at door and seats them

_____ Directs service of guests as needed to meet service standards

_____ Handles guest complaints

_____ Checks on responsible service of alcohol

Supervision of Staff

_____ Reviews all job descriptions

_____ Calculates payroll hours

_____ Schedules staff

_____ Coaches staff

_____ Fills out yearly performance appraisal forms

_____ Holds weekly meetings

_____ Disciplines staff when needed

_____ Interviews applicants

_____ Selects and hires staff

_____ Orients and trains new employees

Fig. 9-5   Continued

Dining Room Maintenance

_____ Completes orders for dining room supplies

_____ Reports dining room repairs

Cost Control

_____ Plans dining room budget

_____ Checks dining room payroll costs against budget and explains any variances

_____ Checks dining room supply costs against budget and explains any variances

General

_____ Dresses according to dress code

_____ Is hospitable and courteous toward guests

_____ Comes to work and is on time

_____ Works as a team member

Please sign below upon completion of training. Both the employee and the trainer certify by their signatures that the training has been adequate to prepare the new employee to function in his or her new position.

_____   _____

Signature/Date (Employee)   Signature/Date (Trainer)

Fig. 9-6 SAMPLE ON-THE-JOB TRAINING CHECKLIST FOR A DINING ROOM ATTENDANT

OJT CHECKLIST—DINING ROOM ATTENDANT

Name of Trainee: _____

Date Starting Training: _____

Trainer(s): _____

Write the date in the blank space next to each task when you feel the trainee has mastered it.

Assists Servers

_____ Sets tables

_____ Folds napkins

_____ Clears a table

_____ Stacks and carries a bus pan

_____ Pours water

_____ Serves bread and butter

_____ Serves coffee and tea

_____ Changes an ashtray

_____ Does sidework

General

_____ Dresses according to dress code

_____ Is hospitable and courteous toward guests

_____ Comes to work and is on time

_____ Works as a team member

Please sign below upon completion of training. Both the employee and the trainer certify by their signatures that the training has been adequate to prepare the new employee to function in his or her new position.

_____   _____
Signature/Date (Employee)   Signature/Date (Trainer)

Fig. 9-7   SAMPLE ON-THE-JOB TRAINING CHECKLIST FOR A COOK

OJT CHECKLIST—COOK

Name of Trainee: _____

Date Starting Training: _____

Trainer(s): _____

Write the date in the blank space next to each task when you feel the trainee has mastered it.

Prepares Food
_____ Uses production sheet
_____ Locates and uses recipes
_____ Adjusts recipes
_____ Gathers necessary supplies
_____ Operates kitchen equipment
_____ Times food preparation
_____ Portions food
_____ Garnishes food
_____ Serves an acceptable product
_____ Keeps written records of all food produced and leftovers
_____ Follows safe food-handling guidelines
_____ Handles leftovers
_____ Cleans and sanitizes work area using cleaning schedule

General
_____ Dresses according to dress code
_____ Is hospitable and courteous toward guests
_____ Comes to work and is on time
_____ Works as a team member

Please sign below upon completion of training. Both the employee and the trainer certify by their signatures that the training has been adequate to prepare the new employee to function in his or her new position.

_____   _____
Signature/Date (Employee)   Signature/Date (Trainer)

Fig. 9-8 SAMPLE ON-THE-JOB TRAINING CHECKLIST FOR A STOREKEEPER

OJT CHECKLIST—STOREKEEPER

Name of Trainee: _____

Date Starting Training: _____

Trainer(s): _____

Write the date in the blank space next to each task when you feel the trainee has mastered it.

Receiving

_____ Verifies actual quantity received against vendor's invoice and purchase order

_____ Verifies price

_____ Spot-checks quality of incoming goods

_____ Discusses with Chef any receiving problems immediately

Storing

_____ Stores foods in appropriate locations

_____ Stores frozen and refrigerated foods quickly

_____ Rotates stock

_____ Cleans storage areas according to cleaning schedule

Record Keeping

_____ Takes physical inventory using inventory book

_____ Issues stock

General

_____ Dresses according to dress code

_____ Is hospitable and courteous toward guests

_____ Comes to work and is on time

_____ Works as a team member

Please sign below upon completion of training. Both the employee and the trainer certify by their signatures that the training has been adequate to prepare the new employee to function in his or her new position.

_____   _____
Signature/Date (Employee)   Signature/Date (Trainer)

can train, it is advisable to compensate that person in some way, because the employee is being asked to take on another significant responsibility. Examples of rewards for trainers include pay increases, a bonus, a new title at a higher level, special privileges, or some mark of distinction, such as a pin.

What characteristics do you nook for in a trainer? The trainer should

Be knowledgeable
Display enthusiasm
Have a sense of humor
Communicate clearly, concisely, and in a straightforward manner
Be sincere, caring, respectful, and responsive toward employees
Encourage employee performance and be patient
Set an appropriate role model
Be organized
Maintain control with employees
Listen well
Be friendly and outgoing
Keep calm and be easygoing
Try to involve all employees
Facilitate the learning process
Positively reinforce employees

When you are orienting new managers, it is a good idea for you to assign another manager who is not in a higher level position, to help the new manager adjust.

COMPANY ORIENTATION

The purpose of company orientation is to give employees an accurate picture of the company, as well as provide them with

An understanding of the corporate culture, values, and goals
A positive attitude toward the company
A sense of belonging to a new group
An understanding of the importance of each job and how it fits into the big picture

When the overall orientation program successfully addresses both job orientation and socialization issues, it can be expected that turnover rates will decrease and that employees will master their new jobs and become part of a team more quickly. Research has shown this to be true.

The corporate culture can be communicated in orientation through the various speakers who model the company's culture and norms, such as the importance of quality service and teamwork. Whereas orientation cannot force employees to care about their new jobs, it can explain what the company wants to accomplish and the employees' role in this.

Company orientation is often done during the first week of a new employee's arrival. When new employees start work, they are normally quite anxious to become competent in handling the many aspects of their new jobs. They will therefore have difficulty hearing the messages of company orientation. So, it is best to conduct company orientation when the new employees feel somewhat comfortable on the job, which would require at least two or three weeks. Also, new employees typically have high expectations when they start a new job, and, after hearing such wonderful things about their new company, their expectations and excitement may become unrealistic, resulting in disappointment and frustration once the job becomes routine.

In smaller foodservice operations, company orientation and job orientation are done together.

Appendix A

Resources

Literacy Programs

ORGANIZATIONS

Business Council for Effective
  Literacy
1221 Avenue of the Americas
  (35th Floor)
New York, NY 10020
(212)512-2415/2412

William F. Delaney
Chief, Research Unit
Employment & Training
  Administration
U.S. Department of Labor,
  Room N-5629
Frances Perkins Building
200 Constitution Avenue, N.W.
Washington, DC 20210
(202)535-0677

Karl Haigler
Director, Division Adult
  Education and Adult
  Literacy Initiative
U.S. Department of Education
400 Maryland Avenue, S.W.
Washington, DC 20202
(202)732-2959

Cheryl Judice
Executive Director
GRASP Adult Learning Center
815 Chicago Avenue
Evanston, IL 60202
(312)328-4420

Peter Waite
Executive Director
Laubach Literacy Action
1320 Jamesville Avenue
Syracuse, NY 13210
(315)422-9121

Dale Yeatts
Research Associate
American Society for Training
  and Development
1630 Duke Street, Box 1443
Alexandria, VA 22313
(703)683-8155

PUBLICATIONS

Duggan, Paula, and Jacqueline Mazza. 1986. *Learning to Work: Improving Youth Employability*. Washington, D.C.: Northeast-Midwest Institute.
Lerche, Renee (ed.). 1985. *Effective Adult Literacy Programs: A Practitioner's Guide*. New York: Cambridge Publishing.

Federal Information Centers

Each state maintains one or more Federal Information Centers, which provide a source of free information on a wide range of government-related topics.

Alabama
Birmingham (205)322-8591
Mobile (205)438-1421

Alaska
Anchorage (907)271-3650

Arizona
Phoenix (602)261-3313
Tucson (602)622-1511

Arkansas
Little Rock (501)378-6177

California
Los Angeles (213)894-3800
Sacramento (916)551-2380
San Diego (619)293-6030
San Francisco (415)556-6600
San Jose (408)275-7422
Santa Ana (714)836-2386

Colorado
Colorado Springs (719)471-9491
Denver (303)234-7181
Pueblo (719)544-9523

Connecticut
Hartford (203)527-2617
New Haven (203)624-4720

Florida
St. Petersburg (813)893-3495
Tampa (813)229-7911

From elsewhere in Florida—
(800)282-8556

Georgia
Atlanta (404)331-6891

Hawaii
Honolulu (808)546-8620

Illinois
Chicago (312)353-4242

Indiana
Gary/Hammond (219)883-4110
Indianapolis (317)269-7373

Iowa
Des Moines (515)284-4448

From elsewhere in Iowa—
(800)532-1556

Kansas
Topeka (913)295-2866

From elsewhere in Kansas—
(800)432-2934

Kentucky
Louisville (502)582-6261

Louisiana
New Orleans (504)589-6696

Maryland
Baltimore (301)962-4980

Massachusetts
Boston (617)565-8121

Michigan
Detroit (313)226-7016
Grand Rapids (616)451-2628

Minnesota
Minneapolis (612)349-5333

Missouri
St. Louis (314)425-4106

For other Missouri locations in
Area Code 314 — (800)392-
7711

Nebraska
Omaha (402)221-3353

From elsewhere in
Nebraska — (800)642-8383

New Jersey
Newark (201)645-3600
Paterson/Passaic (201)523-0717
Trenton (609)396-4400

New Mexico
Albuquerque (505)766-3091
Santa Fe (505)983-7743

New York
Albany (518)463-4421
Buffalo (716)846-4010

New York (212)264-4464
Rochester (716)546-5075
Syracuse (315)476-8545

North Carolina
Charlotte (704)376-3600

Ohio
Akron (216)375-5638
Cincinnati (513)684-2801
Cleveland (216)522-4040
Columbus (614)221-1014
Dayton (513)223-7377
Toledo (419)241-3223

Oklahoma
Oklahoma City (405)231-4868
Tulsa (918)584-4193

Oregon
Portland (503)221-2222

Pennsylvania
Allentown/Bethlehem
(215)821-7785
Philadelphia (215)597-7042
Pittsburgh (412)644-3456
Scranton (717)346-7081

Rhode Island
Providence (401)331-5565

Tennessee
Chattanooga (615)265-8231
Memphis (901)521-3285
Nashville (615)242-5056

Texas
Austin (512)472-5494
Dallas (214)767-8585
Fort Worth (817)334-3624
Houston (713)229-2552
San Antonio (512)224-4471

Utah
Odgen (801)399-1347
Salt Lake City (801)524-5353

Virginia
Newport News (804)244-0480
Norfolk (804)441-3101
Richmond (804)643-4928
Roanoke (703)982-8591

Washington
Seattle (206)442-0570
Tacoma (206)383-5230

Wisconsin
Milwaukee (414)271-2273

State Labor Departments and Human Relations Commissions

Not every state has a Human Relations Commission. If you have a civil rights question and your state has no Human Relations office listed here, ask your state's Department of Labor or the federal Equal Employment Opportunity Commission for assistance.

Alabama
Department of Labor
State Administrative Building,
  Suite 651
Montgomery 36130

Department of Industrial
  Relations
Industrial Relations Building
Montgomery 36130

Alaska
Department of Labor
P.O. Box 1149
Juneau 99802

State Commission for Human
  Rights
421 West Seventh Avenue,
  Suite 101
Anchorage 99501

Arizona
Industrial Commission
800 West Washington Street
P.O. Box 19070
Phoenix 85005

Civil Rights Division
1275 West Washington Street
Phoenix 85007

Arkansas
Department of Labor
1022 High Street
Little Rock 72202

California
Department of Industrial
  Relations
State Building Annex
525 Golden Gate Avenue
San Francisco 94102

Department of Fair
Employment and Housing
1201 I Street, Suite 211
Sacramento 95814

Employment and Development
Department
800 Capitol Mall
Sacramento 95814

Colorado
Department of Labor and
Employment
600 Grant Street, Suite 900
Denver 80203

Civil Rights Commission
1525 Sherman Street, Room 600
Denver 80203

Connecticut
Labor Department
200 Folly Brook Boulevard
Wethersfield 06109

Commission on Human Rights
and Opportunities
90 Washington Street
Hartford 06106

Delaware
Department of Labor
820 North French Street
Wilmington 19801

District of Columbia
Department of Employment
Services
500 C Street, N.W.
Washington 20001

D.C. Office of Human Rights
2000 14th Street, N.W.,
Room 300
Washington 20009

Florida
Department of Labor and
Employment Security
2590 Executive Center Circle,
East
Suite 206 Berkeley Building
Tallahassee 32301

Department of Community
Affairs
2571 Executive Center Circle,
East
Tallahassee 32301

Georgia
Department of Labor
254 Washington Street   .
Atlanta 30334

Hawaii
Department of Labor and
Industrial Relations
830 Punchbowl Street
Honolulu 96813

Idaho
Department of Labor and
Industrial Services
277 North Sixth Street
Boise 83720

Department of Employment
317 Main Street
P.O. Box 35
Boise 83735

Commission on Human Rights
Basement—Statehouse
Boise 83720

Illinois
Department of Labor
310 South Michigan Avenue
Chicago 60604

Fair Employment Practices
Commission
179 West Washington Street,
Fourth Floor
Chicago 60602

Indiana
Department of Labor
100 North Senate Avenue,
Room 1013
Indianapolis 46204-2287

Industrial Board
601 State Office Building
100 North Senate Avenue
Indianapolis 46204

Civil Rights Commission
319 State Office Building
100 North Senate Avenue
Indianapolis 46204

Iowa
Division of Labor Services
100 East Grand Avenue
Des Moines 50319

Iowa Civil Rights Commission
211 East Maple Street
Des Moines 50319

Kansas
Department of Human
Resources
401 Topeka Avenue
Topeka 66603

Commission on Civil Rights
535 Kansas Fifth Floor
Topeka 66603

Kentucky
Labor Cabinet
U.S. 127 South
Frankfort 40601

Commission on Human Rights
P.O. Box 60
Louisville 40203

Louisiana
Department of Labor
1001 North 23rd Street
P.O. Box 94094
Baton Rouge 70804-9094

Office of Labor
5630 Florida Boulevard
P.O. Box 94094
Baton Rouge 70806

Maine
Department of Labor
20 Union Street, Station No. 54
Augusta 04333

Maine Human Rights
Commission
Stevens School Complex,
Station No. 51
Augusta 04333

Maryland
Division of Labor and Industry
Department of Licensing and
Regulation
501 St. Paul Place
Baltimore 21202

Department of Human
Resources
1100 Eutaw Street
Baltimore 21201

Commission on Human
Relations
Metro Plaza
Mondawmin Mall, Suite 300
Baltimore 21215

Massachusetts
Executive Office of Labor
One Ashburton Place,
  Room 2112
Boston 02108

Department of Labor and
  Industry
100 Cambridge Street
Boston 02202

Michigan
Department of Labor
309 North Washington Square
Lansing 48909

Bureau of Employment
  Relations
1200 Sixth Avenue
Detroit 48226

Minnesota
Department of Labor and
  Industry
444 Lafayette Road, Fifth Floor
St. Paul 55101

Department of Human Rights
500 Bremer Tower
Seventh and Minnesota Streets
St. Paul 55101

Mississippi
Employment Security
  Commission
1520 West Capitol
P.O. Box 1699
Jackson 39205

Missouri
Department of Labor and
  Industrial Relations
421 East Dunklin Street
Jefferson City 65101

Montana
Department of Labor and
  Industry
Commissioner's Office
P.O. Box 1728
Helena 59624

Nebraska
Department of Labor
P.O. Box 94600
550 South 16th Street
Lincoln 68509

Equal Opportunity Commission
P.O. Box 94934
301 Centennial Mall South,
  Fifth Floor
Lincoln 68509

Nevada
Office of Labor Commissioner
505 East King Street, Room 602
Carson City 89710

Nevada Equal Rights
  Commission
1515 East Tropicana, Suite 590
Las Vegas 89158

New Hampshire
Department of Labor
19 Pillsbury Street
Concord 03301

New Hampshire Commission
  for Human Rights
66 South Street
Concord 03301

New Jersey
Department of Labor
Labor and Industry Building
John Fitch Plaza
Trenton 08625

Department of Law and Public
  Safety
State House Annex
Trenton 08625

New Mexico
Department of Human Services
PERA Building
P.O. Box 2348
Sante Fe 87503

Human Rights Commission
Bataan Memorial Building,
  Room 303
Santa Fe 87503

New York
Department of Labor
State Office Campus,
  Building 12
Albany 12240

Division of Human Rights
2 World Trade Center
New York 10047

North Carolina
Department of Labor
4 West Edenton Street
Raleigh 27601

North Dakota
Department of Labor
State Capitol Building
Bismarck 58505

Ohio
Department of Industrial
  Relations
2323 West Fifth Avenue
Columbus 43204

Civil Rights Commission
220 Parsons Avenue
Columbus 43215

Oklahoma
Department of Labor
1315 Broadway Place
Oklahoma City 73103

Human Rights Commission
Jim Thorpe Building,
  Room G-11
Oklahoma City 73105

Oregon
Bureau of Labor and Industries
1400 Southwest Fifth Avenue
Portland 97201

Pennsylvania
Department of Labor and
  Industry
Labor and Industry Building
Harrisburg 17120

Pennsylvania Human Relations
  Commission
100 North Cameron Street
Harrisburg 17101

Rhode Island
Department of Labor
220 Elmwood Avenue
Providence 02907

Commission for Human Rights
10 Abbott Park Place
Providence 02903

South Carolina
Department of Labor
3600 Forest Drive
P.O. Box 11329
Columbia 29211-1329

State Human Affairs
  Commission
1111 Belleview Street
Columbia 29211

South Dakota
Department of Labor
700 Governors Drive
Pierre 57501

State Commission on Human
 Rights
State Capitol
Pierre 57501

Tennessee
Department of Labor
501 Union Building, Second
 Floor
Nashville 37219-5385

Tennessee Commission on
 Human Rights
208 Tennessee Building
Nashville 37219

Texas
Department of Labor and
 Standards
Box 12157
Capitol Station
Austin 78711

Utah
Industrial Commission
160 East 300 South
P.O. Box 45580
Salt Lake City 84145-0580

Vermont
Department of Labor and
 Industry
State Office Building
Montpelier 05602

Virginia
Department of Labor and
 Industry
P.O. Box 12064
Fourth Street Office Building
Richmond 23241-0064

Industrial Commission
1000 DMV Drive
Richmond 23220

Washington
Department of Labor and
 Industries
General Administration
 Building
Olympia 98504

State Human Rights
 Commission
1601 Second Avenue Building
Seattle 98101

West Virginia
Department of Labor
Capitol Complex
1800 Washington Street
East Charleston 25305

State Human Rights
 Commission
215 Professional Building
1036 Quarrier Street
Charleston 25301

Wisconsin
Department of Industry, Labor
 and Human Relations
P.O. Box 7946
Madison 53707

Wyoming
Department of Labor and
 Statistics
Herschler Building, Second
 Floor
Cheyenne 82002

Fair Employment Commission
Herschler Building, Second
 Floor
Cheyenne 82002

Recruiting

PUBLICATIONS

Black Resource Guide. Washington, D.C.: R. Benjamin Johnson. Lists organizations, businesses, social organizations, and so on, within the black community.

Cole, K. W. (ed.). 1987. *Minority Organizations.* (3rd ed.) Garrett Park, Md.: Garrett Park Press. Lists organizations serving blacks, Hispanics, American Indians, and Asian Americans. Gives information on job placement activities.

Directory of Executive Recruiters. Fitzwilliam, N.H.: Consultants News. Lists recruiting firms with geographic, industry, and management specialty indexes.

National Professional and Trade Associations of the U.S. Washington, D.C.: Columbia Books.

Recruitment Advertising Guide. Cleveland: Nationwide Advertising Service. Gives circulation and rates of newspapers and magazines.

ORGANIZATIONS

American Vocational
  Association
1210 King Street
Alexandria, VA 22314

Association of Executive Search
  Consultants, Inc.
151 Railroad Avenue
Greenwich, CT 06830

Chamber of Commerce of the
  United States
1615 H Street, N.W.
Washington, DC 20062
(202)659-6000

Cooperative Education
  Association, Inc.
665 15th St., N.W.
Washington, DC 20005

Goodwill Industries of America,
  Inc.
9200 Wisconsin Avenue
Bethesda, MD 20814

National Association of
  Corporate and Professional
  Recruiters
197 Cedarwood Rd.
Stamford, CT 06903

National Association of Private
  Industry Councils
1015 15th Street, N.W.
Suite 600
Washington, DC 20005
(202)289-2950

National Association of
Retarded Citizens
2501 Avenue J
Arlington, TX 76006

National Council on the Aging
600 Maryland Avenue, S.W.
Washington, DC 20024

National Job Training
Partnership, Inc.
1620 Eye Street, N.W.
Suite 328
Washington, DC 20006
(202)887-6020

National Restaurant Association
Handicapped Employment
Program Division
1200 17th Street, N.W.
Washington, DC 20036
(202)331-5900

National Urban League
500 E. 62nd Street
New York, NY 10021

Rehabilitation Services
Administration
330 C Street, S.W.
Washington, DC 20202.
(They can refer you to state
offices of vocational
rehabilitation.)

President's Committee on
Employment of People with
Disabilities
111 20th St., N.W., Suite 636
Washington, DC 20036
(202) 653-5044

U.S. Department of Labor
Employment and Training
Administration
Bureau of Apprenticeship and
Training
Veterans' Employment and
Training
601 D Street, N.W.
Washington, DC 20213

Training

Advantage Media
21601 Marilla Avenue
Chatsworth, CA 91311-4124
(818)700-0504
Provides videotraining
programs in foodservice
sanitation and safety.

American Culinary Federation
P.O. Box 3466
St. Augustine, FL 32084
(904)824-4468
Provides various culinary
publications.

American Management
Association
135 West 50th Street
New York, NY 10020
(212)586-8100
Provides videotraining,
seminars, and books on
management topics.

American Society for Training
and Development
1630 Duke Street
Alexandria, VA 22313
(703)683-8100
Provides general training books
and resource guides.

Council of Hotel and Restaurant
  Trainers
Call the National Restaurant
Association for current address
information.
Has regular meetings.

The Culinary Institute of
  America
Hyde Park, NY 12538
(914)452-9600
Provides videotraining
programs and books.

Educational Foundation of the
  National Restaurant
  Association
250 South Wacker Drive
Chicago, IL 60606
(800)522-7578
(312)715-1010
Provides seminars, certification
courses, and self-development
courses.

Educational Institute of the
  American Hotel and Motel
  Association
P.O. Box 1240
East Lansing, MI 48826
(800)752-4567
(517)353-5527
Provides videotraining
programs, publications, and
seminars.

Foodservice Training Systems
P.O. Box 293
Yardley, PA 19067
(215)493-4988
Provides ready-to-use training
programs, employee handout
materials, and visual aids.

Mark-Maris
2280 Main Street
Buffalo, NY 14214
(716)837-7555
Provides videotraining
programs on various foodservice
topics.

National Educational Media/
  Britannica
310 South Michigan Avenue
Chicago, IL 60604
(800)554-9862
Provides videotraining
programs on various foodservice
topics.

National Restaurant Association
1200 17th Street, N.W.
Washington, DC 20036-3097
(800)424-5156
(202)331-5900
Provides videotraining
programs, publications, and
employee handout materials.

Vocational Media
Box 1050
Mount Kisco, NY 10549-0050
(800)431-1242
Provides videotraining
programs, filmstrips, and slides
on various foodservice topics.

Child-Care Programs

Adolf, Barbara. 1988. *The Employer's Guide to Childcare: Developing Programs for Working Parents.* New York: Praeger.

National Council for Quality Daycare. 1989. *Corporate Sponsored Childcare—Exploring the Options.*

U.S. Department of Labor, Women's Bureau. *Employers and Child Care: Benefiting Work and Family.* Washington, D.C.: Government Printing Office. (This 76-page booklet gives an overview of employers' options in helping employees with child-care needs. It is available by sending a self-addressed mailing label to the address below.)

Women's Bureau
U.S. Department of Labor
200 Constitution Avenue, N.W.
Washington, DC 20210

Appendix B

Duty Statements for Job Descriptions

BAKER

Prepares bread, rolls, muffins, biscuits, cakes, pies, cookies, and so
on, using recipes
Checks production schedule to determine variety and quantity of
goods to bake
Measures ingredients, using measuring cups, spoons, and scales
Mixes ingredients to form dough or batter by hand or using electric
mixer
Prepares dough or batter for cooking
Adjusts drafts or thermostatic controls to regulate oven tempera-
ture and cooking
Removes baked goods from oven and places them on cooling rack

BARTENDER

Mixes and serves alcoholic and nonalcoholic drinks for guests, using
standard recipes
Serves wine and beer
Collects money for drinks served
Orders or requisitions liquors and supplies
Places bottled goods and glasses to make attractive display
Slices and pits fruit for garnishing drinks
Prepares appetizers

CHEF

Supervises, coordinates, and participates in activities of cooks and other kitchen personnel engaged in preparing and cooking foods

Estimates food consumption

Requisitions or purchases food and supplies

Receives and checks food and supplies for quality and quantity

Supervises personnel engaged in preparing, cooking, and serving meat, vegetables, and other foods, using standard recipes

Cooks or otherwise prepares food according to recipe

Portions cooked foods or gives instructions as to size of portions and methods of garnishing

Hires, trains, and discharges kitchen employees

Plans menus

Maintains time and payroll records

DINING ROOM ATTENDANT

Carries dirty dishes from dining room to kitchen

Replaces soiled table linens and sets tables with silverware and glassware

Replenishes supply of clean linens, silverware, glassware, and dishes in dining room

Serves ice water and butter to guests

Cleans and polishes equipment

Makes coffee and fills fruit juice dispensers

FOOD SERVICE SUPERVISOR

Supervises employees in a certain functional area of a foodservice department

Trains employees in methods of performing duties

Assigns and coordinates work of employees

Oversees serving of meals

Oversees cleaning of kitchen, utensils, and equipment

Keeps records, such as amount of meals served and hours worked by employees

Requisitions supplies and equipment to maintain stock levels

Interviews new employees

Maintains payroll records

HOST/HOSTESS

Supervises dining room employees engaged in providing courteous
  and quick service to guests
Greets guests and escorts them to tables
Schedules dinner reservations
Arranges parties for guests
Handles complaints concerning food or service
Hires and trains dining room employees
Schedules employees
Notifies payroll regarding time records

SALAD MAKER

Prepares salads, fruits, melons, and gelatin desserts
Cleans vegetables, fruits, and berries for salads, relishes, and gelatin
  desserts
Mixes ingredients for green salads, fruit salads, and potato salad
Prepares crudité plates
Prepares salad dressings
Prepares cold sandwiches and cheese
^Requisitions supplies daily

WINE STEWARD

Selects, requisitions, stores, sells, and serves wines in restaurant
Keeps inventory and orders wine to replenish stock
Stores wines on racks or shelves
Discusses wine with guests and assists them with selection
Tastes wines prior to serving and serves wines to guests

Appendix C

Checklist for Developing a Training Program

Consider each question below and mark it "yes" or "no" in view of the training needs of your particular situation.

The Goal of the Training
Whether the goal of developing a training program is to conduct initial training, to maintain or upgrade employees' performance, or to retrain for changing job assignments, the goal should be spelled out before the plan for the training program is developed.

_____ Do you want to improve the performance of your employees?

_____ Will you improve your employees by training them to perform their present duties better?

_____ Do you need to prepare employees for newly developed or modified jobs?

_____ Is training needed to prepare employees for promotion?

_____ Is the goal to reduce accidents and increase safety?

_____ Should the goal be to improve employee attitudes, especially concerning waste and spoilage practices?

_____ Do you need to improve the handling of materials in order to break production bottlenecks?

_____ Is the goal to orient new employees to their jobs?

_____ Will you need to teach new employees about overall operations?

_____ Do you need to train employees so that they can help teach new workers in an expansion program?

What the Employee Needs to Learn
Once the goal has been set, the subject matter needs to be determined. The following questions are designed to help you decide what the employee needs in terms of knowledge, skills, and attitudes.

_____ Can the job be broken down into steps for training purposes?
_____ Are there standards of quality which trainees can be taught?
_____ Are there certain skills and techniques which trainees must learn?
_____ Are there hazards and safety practices which must be taught?
_____ Have the methods which employees must use to avoid or minimize waste and spoilage been established?
_____ Are there materials handling techniques that should be taught?
_____ Has the best way for the trainees to operate the equipment been determined?
_____ Are there performance standards which employees must meet?
_____ Are there attitudes that need improvement or modifications?
_____ Will information on the company's services help employees to do a better job?
_____ Will the employee need instruction about departments other than his or her own?

Method of Instruction
There are various methods of instruction, each of which works best in different types of training situations.

_____ Can employees be trained on the job so that they can produce while they learn?
_____ Should classroom training be conducted by a trainer?
_____ Will a combination of scheduled on-the-job training and classroom instruction work best?
_____ Does the subject matter call for lectures or a participative method of teaching?
_____ Does the subject matter lend itself to demonstrations and employee tryouts?
_____ Can the subject matter be simulated in a classroom?

Teaching Materials to Use
Teaching materials help the trainer make points and enables the trainees to grasp and retain the instructions.

_____ Will a training program, including trainer and employee information, be used?

_____ Are there training programs available for purchase in this area?

_____ Will a training program have to be developed?

_____ Are there videocassette programs available which could be used as an adjunct to the program?

_____ Are there pads and easels, videocassette players and monitors, and projectors available for the training?

Physical Facilities Needed
It is important to consider what facilities are available in view of the instructional methods and teaching materials to be used.

_____ If the training is not on the job, is there a conference room or another room in which it can be conducted?

_____ Can the trainer use all of his or her audiovisual aids where the training will take place?

_____ Is there enough seating available?

_____ Should the training be conducted off the premises?

Timing
You need to consider both when the training will occur and how long each session will be.

_____ Should the training be conducted during working hours?

_____ Should the training be held before or after work?

_____ Can the length of each session and the number of sessions be established?

The Trainer
The success of training depends to a great extent on the trainer. A qualified trainer can achieve good results, even with limited resources.

_____ Is there someone who is willing and able to function as the trainer?

_____ Will a trainer have to be trained?

_____ Is there a consultant who could be brought in to train part-time?

Who Should Attend the Training and How to Publicize It
Company policies will help determine who should attend the training sessions. Publicity is important in order to attract good applicants.

_____ Should new employees be hired for training?

_____ Should the training of new employees be a condition of employment?

_____ Are there present employees who need training?

_____ Should employees who want the training in hopes of promotion be considered?

_____ Should training be a condition for promotion?

_____ Will employees be permitted to volunteer for the training?

_____ Will the program be publicized through notices and word of mouth?

Cost of the Program

Before you start the program, it is important for you to estimate its costs.

_____ Is the cost to implement the program affordable?

_____ Will employees be paid for attending the program?

Evaluating the Program

The results of the program need to be evaluated to determine the extent to which the original goal was achieved.

_____ Can the results of the training be checked against the goal or objective?

_____ Can data on trainee performance be developed before, during, and after training?

_____ Will trainees be tested on the knowledge and skills they have acquired?

_____ Will records be kept on the progress of each trainee?

_____ Will the training be followed up by a supervisor?

_____ Should you personally check and control the program?

Bibliography

Cited References

Boyle, Kathy. 1987. Giving employees a share of the business. *Restaurants USA* 7(2):16–19.

Business Council for Effective Literacy. 1987. Job-related basic skills. *BCEL Bulletin* 1(2):1–45.

Carlino, Bill. 1988. The labor crisis: Looking for solutions. *Nation's Restaurant News* May 30:F1, F6, F10.

Copeland, Lennie. 1988. Learning to manage a multicultural work force. *Training* 25(5):49–56.

Denton, D. Keith. 1987. Getting employee commitment. *Management Solutions* 32(10):17–24.

Equal Employment Opportunity Commission. 1974. *Affirmative Action and Equal Employment: A Guidebook for Employers*. Vol. 1. Washington, D.C.: U.S. Equal Employment Opportunity Commission.

Gordon, Elizabeth. 1990. What's being done about child care. *Restaurants USA* 10(2):40–42.

Lee, Chris. 1989. Industry Report: The 3Ds. *Training* 26(10): 67–76.

Lefever, Michael M., and JeAnna Lanza Abbott. 1990. The growing reality of negligent hiring claims: Implications for hospitality law. *Hospitality Research Journal* 14(1):139–142.

Levering, Robert, Milton Moskowitz, and Michael Katz. 1985. *The One Hundred Best Companies to Work for in America*. New York: NAL.

Michalski, Nancy. 1990. Foodservice employment: 11 million by 2000. *Restaurants USA* 10(2):36–37.

National Restaurant Association. 1990. *Foodservice Employers and the Labor Market*. Washington, D.C.: National Restaurant Association.

———. 1989. *Foodservice Employment 2000: Exemplary Industry Program*. Washington, D.C.: National Restaurant Association.

———. 1988. *Foodservice Industry 2000*. Washington, D.C.: National Restaurant Assocation.

———. 1988. *A 1988 Update: Foodservice and the Labor Storage*. Washington, D.C.: National Restaurant Association.

———. 1987. *Non-Traditional Reward Systems for Foodservice Employees*. Washington, D.C.: National Restaurant Association.

Von der Embse, Thomas J., and Rodney E. Wyse. 1985. Those reference letters: How useful are they? *Personnel* 62(1):42–46.

Zemke, Ron. 1989. Employee orientation: A process, not a program. *Training* 26(8):35–38.

———. 1985. Is performance appraisal a paper tiger? *Training* 22(12):24–32.

Other References

Arthur, Diane. 1986. Preparing for the interview. *Personnel* 63(2):37–49.

———. 1986. *Recruiting, Interviewing, Selecting, and Orienting New Employees*. New York: AMACOM.

Baker, Carolyn A. 1988. Flex your benefits. *Personnel Journal* 67(5):54–61.

Bargerstock, Andrew S. 1989. Recruitment options that work. *Personnel Administrator* 34(3):52–55.

Berger, Raymond M. 1987. How to evaluate a selection test. *Personnel Journal* 66(2):88–91.

Besnoff, Larry. 1989. Avoiding claims of negligent hiring. *Supervisory Management* 34(8):11–16.

Broadwell, Martin M. (ed.). 1985. *Supervisory Handbook*. New York: John Wiley.

Brown, Darrel R. 1985. Sharpening your job interviewing techniques. *Supervisory Management* 30(8):29–32.

Business Council for Effective Literacy. 1987. Job-related basic skills: A guide for planner of employee programs. *BCEL Bulletin* 2:1–44.

Carlino, Bill. 1989. Operators tap disabled to ease labor shortage. *Nation's Restaurant News* March 6:1, 66.

———. 1988. The labor crisis: Looking for solutions. *Nation's Restaurant News* May 30:F1, F6, F10.

Cascio, Wayne F. (ed.). 1989. *Human Resource Planning, Employment and Placement*. Washington, D.C.: Bureau of National Affairs.

Cook, Suzanne H. 1988. Playing it safe: How to avoid liability for negligent hiring. *Personnel* 65(11):32–36.

Coppess, Marcia Hibsch. 1988. Temps: Can they help your labor shortage? *Restaurants USA* 8(1):16–18.

Davidson, Jeffrey P. 1986. Checking references. *Supervisory Management* 31(1):29–31.

Dee, Dorothy. 1987. Fringe benefits. *Restaurants USA* 7(10):29–31.

Eliott, Travis. 1983. *Profitable Foodservice Management: Through Job Analysis, Descriptions and Specifications.* Washington, D.C.: National Restaurant Association.

———. 1983. *Profitable Foodservice Management: Through Recruitment and Selection of Employees.* Washington, D.C.: National Restaurant Association.

Evans, Deane. 1988. Rules ban polygraph testing. *Nation's Restaurant News* November 28:47.

Evans, Karen M., and Randall Brown. 1988. Reducing recruitment risk through preemployment testing. *Personnel* 65(9):55–64.

Feuer, Dale. 1987. Coping with the labor shortage. *Training* 24(3):64–75.

Fintel, Julie. 1989. Spotlight on the Americans with Disabilities Act: What the bill means to restaurateurs. *Restaurants USA* 9(11):8–12.

Follin, Mary. 1989. How Foodservice Is Meeting the Childcare Challenge. *Restaurants USA* 9(9):21–23.

Fryar, Carolyn. 1988. Managing fluctuating workloads with temps. *Management Solutions* 33(2):23–27.

Ghorpade, Jaisingh V. 1988. *Job Analysis: A Handbook for the Human Resources Director.* Englewood Cliffs, N.J.: Prentice-Hall.

Glover, Julie Ashworth, and G. Roger King. 1989. Traps for the unwary employer: How to avoid exposure to negligent hiring liability. *Personnel Administrator* 34(7):52–55.

Granrose, Cherlyn S., and Eileen Appelbaum. 1986. The efficiency of temporary help and part-time employees. *Personnel Administrator* 31(1): 71–83.

Grant, Philip C. 1988. What use is a job description? *Personnel Journal* 67(2):44–53.

Griffin, Maura. 1989. The immigration law three years later. *Restaurants USA* 9(9):34–36.

Grossman, Morton E., and Margaret Magnus. 1988. The boom in benefits. *Personnel Journal* 67(11):51–55.

Hanna, John B. 1986. *Managing Employee Benefits.* Fort Worth, Tex.: U.S. Small Business Administration.

Harrison, Jeff. 1990. First impressions: How to market your company to prospective employees. *Restaurants USA* 10(3):33–34.

Hergenrather, Edmund R. 1988. 32 points no interviewer should miss. *Recruitment Today* 1(1):28–32.

Herlong, Joan. 1990. The ABCs of literacy. *Restaurants USA* 10(1):11–15.

Holmes, Steven A. 1990. Rights bill for the disabled sent to Bush. *The New York Times* July 14:6.

Hopkins, Kevin R., Susan L. Nestleroth, and Clint Bolick. 1991. *Help Wanted How Companies Can Survive and Thrive in the Coming Worker Shortage.* New York: McGraw-Hill, Inc.

Hunt, James W. 1988. *The Law of the Workplace: Rights of Employers and Employees*. Washington, D.C.: Bureau of National Affairs.

Hurst, Michael. 1989. Hiring for personality. *Restaurants USA* 9(5)18–20.

Inwald, Robin. 1990. Those "little white lies" of honesty test vendors. *Personnel* 67(6):52–58.

Johns, Horace E., and H. Ronald Moser. 1989. Where has EEO taken personnel policies? *Personnel* 66(9):63–66.

Kennedy, William R. 1987. Train managers to write winning job descriptions. *Training and Development Journal* (41)4:62–66.

King, Paul. 1989. Working with alternatives. *Food Management* 24(3):126–135.

Koch, Jennifer. 1989. Ads with flair. *Personnel Journal* 68(10):46–55.

Kohl, John P., and David B. Stephens. 1989. Wanted: Recruitment advertising that doesn't discriminate. *Personnel* 66(2):18–26.

LaGreca, Genevieve, and Mona Rosenberg. 1987. *A Primer on How to Recruit, Hire and Retain Employees*. Washington, D.C.: National Restaurant Association.

Long, Richard C. 1988. Public records: What's missing from most background checks. *Recruitment Today* 1(1):40–45.

McCool, Audrey C. 1988. Older workers: Understanding, reaching and using this important labor resource effectively in the hospitality industry. *Hospitality Education and Research Journal* 12(2):365–76.

McLauchlin, Andrew. 1990. Stiffer penalties for child-labor violations. *Restaurants USA* 10(4):8–9.

Madison, Roger, and Barbara Knudson-Fields. 1987. The law and employee-employer relationships: The hiring process. *Management Solutions* 32(2):12–20.

Maddux, Robert B. 1988. *Quality Interviewing*. Los Altos, Calif.: Crisp Publications.

Meyer, Robert, and Gerald C. Meyer. 1988. Older workers: Are they a viable labor force for the hotel community. *Hospitality Education and Research Journal* 12(2):361–64.

Miller, Ernest C. 1980. An EEO examination of employment applications. *The Personnel Administrator* 25(3):63–81.

Mills, Susan. 1989. How immigration reform is affecting restaurateurs. *Restaurants USA* 9(9):34–35.

———. 1988. A review of industry health insurance plans. *Restaurants USA* 8(8):42–44.

Mondy, R. Wayne, Robert M. Noe, and Robert E. Edwards. 1986. What the staffing function entails. *Personnel* 63(4):55–58.

National Restaurant Association. 1989. *The Legal Problem Solver for Foodservice Operators*. Washington, D.C.: National Restaurant Association.

———. 1986. *Foodservice and the Labor Shortage*. Washington, D.C.: National Restaurant Association.

National Restaurant Association and Malcolm M. Knapp, Inc. 1989. 1990 National Restaurant Association foodservice industry forecast: Labor trends. *Restaurants USA* 9(11):34–36.

Nerad, Alan J., and Steven H. Werner. 1989. Selecting honest employees without a polygraph test. *Restaurants & Institutions.* December 25:16.

Oberle, Joseph. 1990. Teaching English as a second language. *Training* 27(4):61–67.

Odiorne, George S. 1990. Beating the 1990s' labor shortage. *Training* 27(7):32–35.

Plachy, Roger J. 1987. Writing job descriptions that get results. *Personnel* 64(10):56–63.

Riehle, Hudson. 1989. A review of employee turnover rates for 1988. *Restaurants USA* 9(10):38–39.

Rinella, Sal D. 1989. Burger King hooks employees with educational incentives. *Personnel Journal* 68(10):90–99.

Rosen, Benson, and Thomas H. Jerdee. 1989. Investing in the older worker. *Personnel Administrator* 34(4):70–74.

Ryan, Monnie. 1989. Getting through to them: Behavior-based interviewing. *Restaurants USA* 9(5)18–20.

Scalise, David G., and Daniel J. Smith. 1986. Legal update: When are job requirements discriminatory? *Personnel* 63(3):41–48.

Scollard, Gene F. 1985. Dynamic descriptions. *Management World* 14(5):34–35.

Stanton, Erwin S. 1988. Fast-and-easy reference checking by telephone. *Personnel Journal* 67(11):123–30.

Stone, Florence M. (ed.). 1989. *The AMA Handbook of Supervisory Management.* New York: AMACOM.

Uris, Auren. 1988. *88 Mistakes Interviewers Make and How to Avoid Them.* New York: AMACOM.

VanDyke, Thomas, and Sandra Strick. 1988. New concepts to old topics: Employee recruitment, selection and retention. *Hospitality Education and Research Journal* 12(2):347–60.

Wagel, William H. 1989. Hardee's: One step ahead in the race for employees. *Personnel* 66(4):20–24.

Wehrenberg, Stephen B. 1989. Skill and motivation divide training and orientation. *Personnel Journal* 68(5):111–13.

INDEX